More Praise for *At Your Service*

"'Can't do' or 'Won't do' versus 'Yes, we can' and 'We'd love to.' Thanks for the strong positive ending to this book. It saved me from being depressed by all the people who defeat themselves!"

— *Jack Kahl, Chairman & CEO, Manco Inc.*

"In the retailing of goods and services, it is 'Service! service! service!' and not 'Location! location! location!' Hal Becker's latest book clearly spells out how good service pays and bad service costs. Every retailer should read it."

— *Herb Strawbridge, former CEO,*
Higbee's/Dillard's Department Stores

"Hal Becker is mad as hell and is not going to take it any more. He shows America how the customer should be in control. If not, is your business in control? *At Your Service* is fun and easy to read. We can all benefit by understanding customer service through the eyes of Hal Becker."

— *Stephen M. Shapiro, President, Cellular*
Communications Puerto Rico

AT YOUR SERVICE

AT YOUR SERVICE

Calamities, Catastrophes, and Other Curiosities of Customer Service

HAL BECKER

John Wiley & Sons, Inc.

New York • Chichester • Weinheim • Brisbane • Singapore • Toronto

Library of Congress Cataloging-in-Publication Data:

Becker, Hal M.
    At your service: calamities, catastrophes, and other curiosities
of customer service / Hal Becker.
        p.   cm.
    Includes index.
    ISBN 0-471-25542-4 (pbk. : alk. paper)
    1. Customer services.   2. Customer relations.   I. Title.
HF5415.5.B432   1998
658.8'12—dc21

Printed in the United States of America.

10   9   8   7   6   5   4   3   2   1

I dedicate this book
to the memory of my parents

and to my relatives and my good friends,
who have taken on the role of my parents,

giving me the strength
to live life and have fun.

Preface

My passport was about to expire, so I went to the post office and got the form to renew my passport. On the form, it said I must send in my original passport.

That was a problem for me because unexpected trips come up, and I didn't see how I could be without my passport for a whole month or so. I looked on the form and saw a phone number to call.

When I dialed it, a machine said, "If you would like to talk to an automated operator, it will be 35 cents a minute. If you would like to talk to a live attendant, it will be $1.05 a minute." The nonhuman voice also said to call between 8 A.M. and 8 P.M. Eastern time, Monday through Friday, excluding federal holidays.

I cannot talk to anybody at the State Department unless I pay for it. Is this where my tax money goes? I just want to ask a human being a question, but it's not possible.

So I dedicate this book to the U.S. government, which gave me one of my favorite customer service stories.

Postscript

I wasn't the only one furious about this 900 number. On September 28, 1997, I was delighted to read in my daily newspaper that the House of Representatives voted to close the State Department's 900 passport telephone line that requires us taxpaying citizens to pay for information we used to get for free.

Sponsors said the 900 line was a form of double taxation and that the State Department should be prohibited from using a pay-for-service telephone line to communicate with constituents.

Acknowledgments

To Florence Mustric, whose genius makes me look like a real author.

To Connie Atkins, who types faster than I talk.

To David Licker, my accountant, who really did nothing, but I promised I would mention him.

To Jon Lief, who made up the Customer Behavior Test in the back of this book and whose creative genius helped me.

To 5th Wave, for allowing me to give them money for their wonderful cartoons.

To all my friends, who put up with my complaining about the small stuff over the past four years.

To Larry Kurlander, whose kindness and generosity will never be forgotten, because he keeps reminding me.

To Neil Gurney, my friend and guide throughout life, who has kept me focused and headed always in the right direction.

To Holly and Nicole, who have added much balance and incredible love to my life.

To Bob Shook, a great advisor, a great mentor, and a great friend.

To Roger Herman, one of the greatest publishers, authors, and speakers (yeah, he does it all and very well).

To Mike Hamilton, the other greatest publisher, who made me make this book my second child.

Acknowledgments

To Gary Lieberman, whom I've known since the sixth grade, and with each year that passes, he impresses me more with his incredible knowledge and clear thinking.

To Jeff Herman, who put the deal together . . . and I will owe him favors for the rest of my life.

To Hillard Lazarus, the greatest oncologist, who saved my life in 1983 and gave me a second chance to do it right.

Contents

Contents

Introduction

This is a compilation of events that all happened to me personally over the past four years. I am telling you exactly what happened *and* what should have happened. These episodes are factual with no embellishments. The names, locations, and a number of identifying facts about the companies and their employees have been changed.

This book is created out of a love and respect for the service industry, *not* out of hate.

Years ago the book *The Incredible Journey* was written about two dogs and a cat that traveled across the country to be reunited with their owners. Well, it's an incredible journey to find great service.

There was a reason why those dogs and that cat had to make their journey, but there's no excuse why we humans should have to go to such lengths to find great service. Outstanding companies are the exception, not the norm. This is wrong!

Only a few companies give exceptionally great service, and I'll mention outstanding examples of them later in this book. It drives me nuts that I should have to go to such extremes to squeeze decent or even average service out of so many companies.

It also drives me bananas (my doctor said I should eat more fruit) that so many people put up with poor or average service—and that so many people don't realize that they *should* be able to get decent service.

In essence, we constantly get poor service, not good service! And when we do get good service, we are amazed. I think it should be just the opposite. But most people who provide customer service just don't get the message. They keep giving us lip service.

So with this book I'm trying to send a message. This book is a slice of one guy's story of poor service from many different providers and a lesson in what each company should have done to correct that poor service.

If you own, manage, or work in any of the businesses or industries mentioned in this book, I hope you don't take offense. First, I'm sure you have a great many positive stories to tell.

And second, whether or not your company is in this book, I sincerely hope you will learn something about what not to do and what *to* do. In fact, by the time you get halfway or so through this book, you should be anticipating what I'm going to say.

One more thing: It's really easy and fun to be nice and to go out of your way to please the customer. Just try it—you'll like it!

The Good Old Days

What a great world it would be if we could go back to 1936 and live in the era in which we had the general store. When you walked in, the owner knew you and greeted you by name. Everything was personal, and the store had an account for you. The owner simply wrote down what you owed on a little piece of paper.

No computers, no electronics. Today we have automation, computerization, and depersonalization. It's all supposed to make things easier, faster, and more accurate, but we have lost the personal touch.

Automation and computerization have made business impersonal. Employees are trained on using the equipment, *not* on interpersonal skills. Employees learn how to operate the cash register or the computer, *not* how to greet and help customers. It doesn't have to be that way!

I go wild when I call up a company and say, "Is so-and-so in?" and the response is, "I'm sorry, he (or she) is away from his (or her) desk." It amazes me that people now are too lazy or are trained not to look for someone rather than say, "Please hold on," rather than say, "May I page him for you?" People just say, "He's away from his desk." In my mind I picture that the person I need to talk to is just around the corner having a conversation with someone.

What I do in this situation is say, "Excuse me, can you go locate him or can you page him?" I have to give them instructions on what to do. I don't like giving instructions. I just want to talk to the person that I called.

This problem is becoming worse and worse. Before we had voice mail, people would go find someone for you. They would say, "Hold on while I go get him for you." If I am going to the trouble to make a call, I want to talk to a human being. I don't want voice mail!

Technology has made people lazy. They just want to do the easy thing and say, "I'm sorry, he's away from his desk." I would not stand for this response if it were my company.

Here's another thing. In the old days there were fewer people, and life moved at a reasonable pace. Now we just rush through life and do everything as fast as possible.

Years ago, we went into a restaurant, sat down, and ordered a meal. Then came Fast Food, followed by Faster Drive-Through food. Now we have Really Fast Food, where they just throw hamburgers at you as you drive by—you can't even stop.

Look at Federal Express or UPS. The fastest-growing segment of their business is not overnight delivery—it's now *same-day* delivery. We *all* need to slow down a little bit, relax, and devote more time to providing better service, not lip service.

The incidents in this book are all my personal experiences, things that happened to me. They are without embellishments—all 100% true!

In some cases, the incident reported in this book was one negative experience with a company that previously had provided me dozens or even hundreds of positive experiences. In some cases in which I had a terrible experience, I never went back to that company again, but in other cases I went back because I knew the bad experience was an aberration.

Do my experiences mean that these companies are bad to all people? Of course not! Many of these corporations are still great service providers and fine corporations.

Every one of us has experienced poor customer service. The key to this book is to laugh a little, have some fun reading the stories, *and then* ask yourself, "What insight does this book give me? What can I do in the company where I am the owner, manager, or employee so that things like this happen less and less often?"

I also believe people need training on how to be a customer. I am always amazed at how many people accept poor service and keep going back for more. No matter what your personal style, I hope this book gets you thinking about ways to approach a manager or owner to get the service that you deserve. We can reinforce the positive and try to change the negative!

I am sure it's impossible to have 100% customer satisfaction in every business on every encounter. But if each day we get as close as possible to 100%, the world would be much better for business and for consumers.

We the customers would get less frustrated and we wouldn't get so angry. We would be more loyal to more companies. In this better world, L.L. Bean, Lexus, Nordstrom's, and Ritz-

Carlton would not be exceptions. Many more companies would provide outstanding customer service. That is my hope.

Why I Wrote This Book

When I sit down at dinner with friends, I always have a story to tell about the terrible customer service I experienced that day. What happens when I do this? Instantly my friends break in: "Wait! Let me tell you about what happened to *me* today!" These things happen to all of us. They drive us all a little crazy.

So I decided to collect some of these events—the incredible, the trivial, and the ridiculous—and put them in a book so we can all have a few chuckles.

In the next-to-last chapter I have included examples of some of the best companies in the world and what they have done to ensure customer service. I don't want this book to be negative. I want to dedicate it to the best customer service in the world.

And in the last chapter, I talk about the future, about where I see the customer-service revolution headed.

The Customer Is Always . . .

What is the expression we always hear? "The customer is always right." Wrong! That is probably one of the least true things ever said. The customer is almost *never* right. The customer is usually wrong.

But the customer is *in charge*. If you say no to a customer, you will lose that customer. In my stories, the customer was never in charge. In all these instances, the company policy was in charge; or mismanaged, uninformed, stupid people were in charge.

In these next pages, I want to show you how simple it is to have incredible customer service. In my opinion, the next few decades will be the era of customer service, when the best companies will win by providing exceptional service.

We are all starting to sell "me-too" products. In other words, there's not much difference out there between the products or services that different companies offer. Whatever your company has or does, a competitor probably has or does the exact same thing. What differentiates the best companies in the world today is their service. They don't give lip service— they give true customer service.

A few years back I had my first chance at being—or attempting to be—an entrepreneur. In 1979, after having three American cars stolen, I bought my first import, a Honda. Soon afterward, I received a follow-up call to see if I was satisfied with my experience in the dealership's service department. Boy, was I impressed by that call!

So I called the owner to thank her for the call and to ask her a few questions about what was, at least to me, a novel concept. The owner explained that the dealership had people working part-time making these calls to check the level of customers' satisfaction.

Right then lights went off in my head, and I thought, "Wow! I have to start a business like this!" I did about eight months of research, and the only company I could find that did such customer satisfaction follow-up was a small company in Louisville, Kentucky.

So, on December 1, 1982, I opened Direct Opinions, Inc., with one employee and no clients. To make a long story short, we paid our telemarketers 45 cents per call and charged our clients 85 cents per completed call. In 1990, when I decided to sell the company, we were conducting more than 2 million calls in nine cities throughout the United States and Canada. I was told that we were the largest U.S. company doing follow-up telephone calls. Whether or not that's true, we sure got a great inside look at the world of customer service!

I want to stress a very important thing. I view problems as *creative opportunities*. Why? Because when your customers have a problem, you can take action to correct their problem. At that point you have the opportunity to take better care of them than anyone else can. If you really blow away your customers with incredible service, they will want to stay with you. They know that you will always take care of them, and they will tell other people about your great service. As you read this book you will notice that all the names are changed to reflect either nonexisting or fictitious companies and their employees. My Intent is for the reader to enjoy the book, laugh a little, possibly identify with the event, and most important, realize what great service is all about and then what to do to correct a situation with regard to poor customer service.

I hope you enjoy reading *At Your Service*. I had a lot of fun writing this book. At the same time, I have a serious message. It's my hope that together—as owners, employees, and consumers—we all can work to change the situation so that stories of poor customer service become the exception, not the norm.

AT YOUR SERVICE

1 I Gotta Write This Book

PRINTO'S

You can thank Printo's for this book. When this incident happened to me, I decided I had to write *At Your Service*.

* * * *

"Yes, good morning, Hal Becker. This is Steve at Printo's. It's about 1:40 in the morning on Sunday. The reason I'm calling, sir, is you left a job with us for business cards to be run. We have looked the job over, and we feel our machines are inadequate to do the precise job that you need.

"Now, we have no problem with trying to help you out on this job. Our other store has a Xerox 5100 [*or 5900—I couldn't tell—as if it made a difference to me*], and it should be capable of running the cards for you. Their number, in case you want to call them, is 555-2679. If our other store cannot help you with this, then we suggest you try a printer, mainly because your job has such exacting requirements.

"I'm sorry to have to call you, but this is what we feel, and we'd rather you have a professional printer do the job for you than for us to do it and you not be happy with it. I will be here until 8:00 A.M. on Sunday morning.

"So, if you want to call me, please feel free. The other person to talk to is Mary Ann. She is the daytime supervisor here, and she will be in tomorrow on Sunday from 8:00 in the morning until 4:00 in the afternoon. Thank you."

I was dead asleep when he left that message on my voice mail. This guy called at 2:00 A.M. That's right, 2 A.M.

Let me go back to the beginning. I went to Printo's and dropped a job off at 4:00 on Friday afternoon.

Now, Printo's did this job the first time, and they already had reprinted it twice. The card is straightforward. It's one color, dark blue, printed on both sides. No embossing, nothing fancy. Just a simple down-to-earth card. They have done this very same job three times for me.

I said, "When will my job be ready?"

They said, "At 5:00 tomorrow afternoon."

So the next day, Saturday, I called them at 5:00 P.M. Before I drove there, I wanted to be absolutely sure that my job was ready.

They said, "Oh, I'm sorry, we couldn't get it done." They just hadn't gotten around to it. "Call back at 8:00 this evening."

I said, "It has to be done. I need to have this before tomorrow." To tell the truth, I could have waited another day, but I could tell they needed a deadline. I had visions of this job stretching out for weeks.

At 8:00 that evening I called.

The woman who answered the phone said, "I'm sorry, we can't get your job done because our paper cutter isn't working."

I said, "That's not my problem."

She said, "Well, there's another Printo's a few miles from here. You could take it to that Printo's."

The key word here is *you*. Now I was really angry.

I said, "No, *you* could take it to that Printo's."

(What can you do on a Saturday night when you don't feel like going out and there's nothing worth watching on television? You can still find excitement. Printo's is open around the clock. I have no life.)

Sure enough, a couple hours later, at 10:00 P.M., the phone rang. Printo's.

A guy's voice said, "I'm sorry, we can't do your job."

After I yelled at him and took his head off, I said, "You will get this job done. I need it. I'm the customer. If you have to run to the other Printo's, you can do it."

I went to bed. At 2:00 A.M. Saturday night (or Sunday morning, however you look at it), the message above was left on my machine. Okay, guys. That's how you want to play? Fine.

4

I taped the message Printo's had left on my voice mail. In the morning I went to Printo's to talk to the manager and let them know how I felt about all this.

I asked to go into her office, because I believe nobody should ever be criticized in front of other people. I played this tape for her.

She said, "No problem, I'll take care of it."

My job was supposed to be ready on Monday at 11:00 A.M. This time I didn't call them first. I figured that if the manager said, "I'll take care of it," she would see that it got done.

Well, guess what? When I went to pick up my job, it still was not ready. Finally, at 11:40 A.M., I got my cards. They were done right. Printo's charged me full price, but they gave me an extra 1,000 cards.

But Printo's has great customer service. They have a plaque on their wall that says so. It reads, "We are 100% committed to customer service." Somehow I don't think so.

☑ What Should Be Done?

First of all, they should *not* have called me at 2:00 A.M. They may be open around the clock, but they need to remember that 99% of the population, excluding insomniacs, is asleep at that hour. What if I had a sick relative, and the phone rang in the dead of the night? "Printo's."

Second, they told me their problem was that their paper cutter was down. The workers should have just driven my job over to the nearest location, which was about four miles away, about a seven-minute drive, especially at 1:00 A.M. They should have cut it and brought it back.

Third, after all this time has gone by, they tell me the job is beyond the capabilities of their machines. Now, I had this job done three times previously by Printo's. In fact, they are the ones who set it up and did it the first time! If they had looked

The 5th Wave
By Rich Tennant

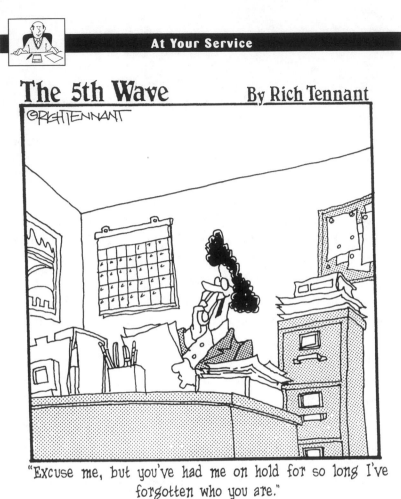

@RICHTENNANT

"Excuse me, but you've had me on hold for so long I've forgotten who you are."

at the receipt I showed them, they would have seen this fact for themselves. Ideally, they would have kept records, and the job order would have shown that they had done this job for me in the past.

They should have gone ahead and had it cut themselves. That way, when I arrived at 8:00 the next morning, they would have it all done, and they would say, "We're so sorry for the inconvenience. This job is on us."

Or another option would have been to give me a coupon good for $50 off my next job, something to make me want to go back again, something to compensate for their poor service and for the repeated inconveniences to me. Instead, they tried to put the monkey on my back and make me do their work—to pick up my job from them and take it to another Printo's.

But the part that was most frustrating was the lack of managing on the part of the manager (you will hear me talk quite a lot about this subject). Sure, it's easy to say, "I'm sorry," or "I'll get it right." But she did nothing right. In fact, she inconvenienced me most of all by making me wait around for the order when it was finally supposed to be completed.

Because the manager did not exceed my expectations and because she did not do something to make me feel special, I have no reason to want to return. The manager's job is to lead her team by example. Because her example was so poor, the team will suffer also. Always remember to lead by example.

2 Getting Here and There

ONE OF THE FIRST LISTINGS IN THE PHONE BOOK, WHERE YOU GET TRAVEL STUFF AT

Since my first book came out, my travel schedule has more than doubled, and I am on airplanes every week. For a few months I went through the usual high-impact aerobic workout: running down the concourse to the gate, carrying my clothes crusher, rushing onto the plane, and cramming my luggage into the tiny compartment above my seat.

Then I noticed that *every* flight attendant and pilot had a suitcase on wheels. So I said to a flight attendant, "What's the deal here? Are those things really that good?" After she gave me a ten-minute demonstration and a look at her uncrushed wardrobe, it became evident to me that I needed my own set of wheels.

The next day I went to a few discount stores. I became totally confused because of all the different types of luggage. In the meantime, I had to go to this travel store for a road map. When I walked in, I noticed a luggage section in the corner. There was a box on wheels, and it cost only $79 instead of the $149 everyone else wanted. My search had ended!

Two weeks and three trips later, my luggage broke. The rubber foot, which enabled the luggage to stand upright, fell off. Hey, no problem. I have my receipt, and it says that if I have any problems or defects within 30 days, I can get a refund or a replacement.

It was a sunny day, so I was in a good mood as I waited in line with my broken baggage. I explained my problem to the woman at the counter.

She said, "I'm sorry, we cannot help you. You have to send it back to the manufacturer." And she tossed me a manufacturer's warranty policy.

I said, "But your receipt says . . ."

She said, "I am sorry. I don't care what it says. That's not our policy."

Okay, I thought. "Get me the manager."

She said, "I'm in charge."

I said, "Yeah, and I'm Ralph Nader. Now get me the manager!"

I waited about 12 minutes for the manager.

She said, "What's the problem?"

I told her.

She said, "Did you get the manufacturer's warranty policy?"

I tried again.

But she repeated, "It's not our policy."

I could see that being rational wasn't working. It was time to act like a jerk.

I said, "Look. This receipt has your logo and address on it. This is a legal binding contract, and if you don't honor it in eight seconds, I will walk across the street to our municipal court and file a suit in small claims court. Now read the bottom of your receipt, especially the part about returns within 30 days!"

She said, "Well, if you are going be *that* way about it," and she replaced my defective luggage.

☑ What Should Be Done?

Wow! Imagine if we were in the land of "Hey, No Problem, Sir (or Ma'am)." The employee's attitude would be, "We are here to serve you, and our only goal is to make you happy, not just so you will buy more stuff from us, but because we want you to enjoy coming in for anything you need, from booking a trip to buying a map. My name is Ms. Nice, and here is my card."

The clerk should have said, "Do you have your receipt? No problem, we will have a new bag for you in a couple minutes. It might take a few minutes to get a new bag for you. Would you like a cup of coffee or a soft drink or anything else while you wait? As long as you're here, would you like a few brochures to help in planning your next business trip or vacation?"

Now isn't this a more positive approach? Doesn't this clerk take a more proactive stance? This approach is really more enjoyable for the employee, as opposed to being defensive and combative. Don't be afraid to try this approach. It works wonders!

Five weeks later my luggage broke again. So I went to a real luggage store and bought one for $189. It is still rolling.

FRUGAL RENT-A-CAR

rented a car, a 1996 Mercury Sable. Actually, an organization rented it for me while I was in Missouri to conduct a seminar for them. I was driving from St. Louis to Springfield, and I was about 50 miles from Springfield when the needle went way past hot. I pulled off the road, looked at my car rental contract, and found the number to call for repairs.

They told me to hold. I held for a long time. Then I hung up and called back—collect, of course. When I got a human being, I explained my problem.

He said, "Just drive the car to Springfield."

I said, "Well, it's about 50 miles away, and I might toast the engine. It's overheating badly."

He said, "Well, that's what you should you do."

I said, "Are you sure you don't want to come get me?"

He said, "No."

I said, "What's your name?"

He said, "Tom." I wrote "Tom" on my contract because I can't remember people's names.

Well, I got to Springfield, and I called the local Frugal office. The woman who answered put me on hold. I waited and waited.

She finally came back on the line and said, "Well, we have to authorize that this is our car."

I said, "No, I will give you my contract number."

She said, "Well, I'm sorry, this has to be authorized before we can give you another car."

I said, "Well, how long will it take to get another car?"

She said, "We have to authorize this first."

I was so mad that I said, "Get me someone else!"

The next person I talked to said I'd have another car in 30 minutes. A man and woman brought the car out, and they couldn't have been nicer. I tried to open the hood on the first car so they could see how the engine had overheated. I couldn't get it open—and neither could they!

"That's okay," they said. "No problem."

When I got back to the Frugal Rent-a-Car office in St. Louis to drop the second car off, I told them I had a little problem. The young woman behind the counter acted as if she was doing me a favor to wait on me.

After I had given her a rundown on all my problems, I said, "What can you do for me?"

She said, "Let me make a phone call." After the call, she said, "I can get you 10% off."

I said, "That's an insult. That's nothing. You inconvenienced me for at least three hours, and on top of that I had a scary ride to Springfield, worrying that I would blow up the engine."

She said, "Well, let me call Tom back." I wondered if Tom, the Thomas Jones who was head of customer service, was the same Tom I had talked to. She said, "I can get you another 5%. I can get you 15%."

I immediately pulled out a copy of my first book, *Can I Have Five Minutes of Your Time?* and wrote inside the cover, "Tom, obviously you know nothing about customer service. You have insulted me more than you have helped me."

She wouldn't even give me back my copy of my contract from the Springfield office. I literally grabbed it out of her hand and left.

I thought, "Rather than write to the president of Frugal, I'll go upstairs now, where the car rental companies have their airport offices. I'll ask for the highest supervisor I can find and tell her the whole story. She'll probably take Thomas Jones apart, which I hope she does. And then maybe he'll go on a singing career."

Frugal Rent-a-Car finally gave me a free day of rental, but only after I practically begged for it. The funny part is that I wasn't even the one paying for the car. It was billed to the organization that hired me.

☑ What Should Be Done?

When my car overheated and I called the office, they should have said, "No problem. We can come get you, or you can drive the car in, whichever you prefer."

They should have had a computer system that, when I got back to the St. Louis office, alerted them that I'd had a problem. They should have offered me something that would make me want to come back. After I practically got down on my knees and begged, they offered to give me all of 15%—that's $5, folks—when they really should have offered me a day's free rental.

In today's world of so much business and leisure travel, wouldn't you think that at least *one* company would want all my business? The car-rental rates are all pretty close, except for an occasional special promotion in some cities. If one company would be loyal to me and would make me feel important, I certainly would be loyal to that company!

I'm not talking about having one more plastic card with my name on it. I'm not talking about a computer printout with my confirmation number on it so I can avoid waiting in line, although that's a good start.

I *am* talking about a great middle and end. The car-rental company of my dreams might upgrade my car each time I rent. Or the people would take an interest in me instead of in gasoline or additional insurance.

Every business really needs to take a step back, look at itself from the other side of the counter, and ask, "What would it take for me to rent or buy from my own company?" Fill customers' wants, not just their needs. Always ask yourself, "What would I want if I were a customer here?"

And one more thing. I shouldn't have had to practically arm wrestle their staff in order to hang onto my contract!

FRUGAL RENT-A-CAR (AGAIN!)

Well, I did something really stupid. When I dropped the car off, I left my jacket—a beautiful suede jacket—in the trunk. I called Frugal and talked to a guy named Eric. He said, "No problem, we will mail it to you."

A week went by. Nothing. When I called Frugal again, I was told, "Jack didn't tell Angela." I talked to Angela.

She said, "The only way we can mail it is C.O.D."

This was the moment of truth, when it was time to say, "Let-me-talk-to-the-manager-please." I had to talk to someone important, because C.O.D. is out of the question. C.O.D. is like

Russian roulette. There are lots of days when I'm not home, so I knew C.O.D. would be impossible.

As soon as I asked for the manager, I was put on hold—really, the hold button should be renamed the *ignore* button. I hung on there for more than 10 minutes. Finally, someone named Joy came on the line, and I went through my story.

She said, "Well, for every 10 customers, 8 leave something in the car. We would spend at least $1 million a month if we took care of all our customers."

Does this person really think that I'm going to believe this idiotic statistic that she made up on the spot?

I couldn't believe it. I called their customer service, a toll-free number, and they said, "No problem." It took about four or five days before they sent me my jacket. But I had to go through all that runaround, until I finally talked to customer service, and they took care of it.

☑ What Should Be Done?

It should be easy to handle this problem right. It would be easy if people at the lower levels were allowed and trained and expected to solve problems for customers.

The company needs to set the policy that "The customer comes first. Do whatever it takes. Just document it, and document it simply—one form. And, yeah, one more thing: Be nice to the customer." That should be the first rule: "Don't argue with a customer."

And if the company's people need to throw around fun facts that I really don't care about, they should at least be accurate. Every employee should have a cheat sheet that can hang on the cubicle wall next to the mission statement. On second thought, employees can tape the cheat sheet over the mission statement, because it's usually just a lot of gobbledygook that nobody pays any attention to.

This episode is a good example of how one person repre-sents the entire organization and can screw things up so com-pletely that the company loses a customer for life. And here's the scary part: I guarantee that after this incident happened no-body heard about it, which means that no corrective measures could be taken—for me or the next customer.

The central office knew what good customer service was, and top management should make sure that every manager and every employee knows what to do—and does it.

If people *do* leave a lot of personal items behind, then the company has a great opportunity to find a way to take care of its customers and to make it easy for them to get their belong-ings back. This is what I call a *creative opportunity.* As I said in the introduction, this is a chance to impress customers and to keep them coming back.

Imagine what it would be like to own the customer! You go out of your way to take care of them, and the next time they rent a car, they want to use your company again.

Car-rental companies are so competitive. But by not being customer focused, they are saying they don't want my repeat business. Or yours.

PRIMADONNA TRUCKING

I have limited experience dealing with trucking companies. In fact, the only time I have dealt with them is when I have had my books shipped. As I write *At Your Service,* I have had nine printings of my first book, *Can I Have Five Minutes of Your Time?* (I hope you noticed my plug for my first book!)

Being the entrepreneur that I am, I try to get as many routes of distribution as possible for my books in addition to the bookstores. So, at the time of every printing, I order 5,000 copies from my publisher. I sell my books at my seminars, and I have opened a toll-free number to my old company, Direct Opinions, so it can distribute my books, too. I like to keep a large quantity of books on hand so I can distribute them the best way I feel possible.

So I have had nine printings, and nine dealings with trucking companies. I have learned that with these companies, I need what I call the bureau-of-motor-vehicles mentality. Let me explain what I mean.

When you need a new license tag or driver's license, where else can you go? Nowhere. "Wait in line over there. Is it too slow? Too bad. Are you unhappy with how I work? Too bad. You can't fire me because I'm a state employee. I can be as nasty as I want because I have a job for life."

That's how I feel when I deal with trucking companies. They don't care one bit about me. In a few cases the drivers were nice, really good guys. When they were, they always complained about the company.

Never, in my first nine experiences with trucking companies, did I find even one person who was positive about the company and said, "This is the best company I have ever worked for. We really are team players."

Instead, they always have an excuse, or they are passing the buck. These companies have virtually no teamwork. There is always a combative situation rather than a positive one.

Back to this company, Primadonna Trucking. They were delivering my book, *Can I Have Five Minutes of Your Time?* (If you haven't read it yet, don't you think it's time?) Well, let me clarify that. Primadonna Trucking is one of many companies that have delivered my book.

Each time a new printing of the book arrives, it goes through a different local trucking company. So you can imagine that my delivery is not exactly the bread and butter of that local trucker. It's more like a crumb, a stale crumb.

Maybe a trucking company sees me as very small potatoes. But the mark of a really good service company is that it treats all its customers as important. It knows that a small account today may grow into a big one in the future.

Primadonna Trucking is lucky. They got into *At Your Service* because they are the company that made the delivery while I was gathering stories for this book.

Well, here I was, waiting for another shipment of my books to be delivered. Primadonna said the delivery would be at noon. Remember, I'm a one-man operation, and I was waiting in my house for 5,000 books to arrive in 78 cartons that weighted a total of almost 3,000 pounds. I had hired two guys to show up at noon, and I was paying them each $10 per hour.

Primadonna said they would deliver by 12:00 noon. Well, I had to have the two guys there, ready and waiting, but I wasn't exactly holding my breath waiting for the truck to roll into my street.

At 1:00 P.M., no books. At 2:00 P.M. still no books. At 3:00 P.M., *still* no books.

Every hour, I called Primadonna.

Finally Debbie said, "The driver will be there shortly, at 3:30 P.M." All this time, the two guys I'd hired were just sitting around, doing nothing, each of them collecting $10 an hour.

Finally, I called and talked to the dispatcher, who said, "Oh, the driver had to come back to our terminal in Richfield, and then he's going back to your place in Mayfield Heights. He will get to your house around 5:00 P.M. or so."

Richfield, by the way, is in the next county. It's out in the country.

This is unbelievable. Unbelievable! Primadonna doesn't have the decency to take care of me properly. They don't even have the decency to call me!

This is how trucking companies work—at least the ones I have dealt with Correction: this is how they *don't* work.

☑ What Should Be Done?

At the very least, they should have stayed in touch with me. They should have let me know what was going on.

They should have said, "I'm sorry." They should have offered to discount the bill 10% to apologize for all the inconvenience and to indicate that the would like me to use their company again. I would never want to use a company like this again.

Imaging this scenario: The dispatcher calls me and says, "Mr. Becker, this is Debbie from Primadonna Trucking. We have a tiny problem, so we want to call you and tell you the situation. Our truck is running late, and we will get to you an hour late. We are so sorry. Is there anything we can do to help you out in this situation?"

Next, wouldn't it be wonderful if the driver would also be apologetic? It would almost be as if the dispatcher and the driver are on the same team. They both care . . . Maybe even the entire company could care.

Here's a way-out thought. Imagine if Ritz-Carlton had a trucking company. How would their drivers act? How clean would the trucks be? Would they ever run late? And if they did, do you think they would try to earn your business again?

PRIMADONNA TRUCKING (AGAIN!)

I know you're saying, "Is this Becker guy stupid, or what? He had one bad experience, so why would he tempt fate a second time?" The answer is simple. The situation was out of my control. My publisher set up all the delivery schedules, and when I found out the same company was delivering my book again, it was to late to do anything about it.

First, we had to go a couple of rounds back and forth just to settle on a delivery time. Well, we didn't really settle on a time. They finally agreed to make the delivery between 1:00 P.M. and 4:00 P.M.

When it got to be 4:00 P.M., I called Primadonna to tell them the truck hadn't shown up. I called a couple of times before the truck finally rolled in at 5:30 P.M., but the only response I got was, "There's nothing we can do about it." Not an apology, nothing. Just, "Hey, this is the way it goes."

I told Primadonna Trucking that I had a couple of guys waiting at my place to unload the books. I was paying them each $10 an hour, and that meant I was shelling out $100 for these guys just to hang out all afternoon.

When the truck finally arrived at 5:30 P.M. and the guys started to unload my books, the driver said, "Come on! I'm in a hurry. I'm running late." He actually said that! I said, "Look, buddy, I've been waiting for four and a half hours." Here he was telling me he's running late. I wasn't about to hurry up!

When the guys had finished unloading my 78 cases, the pallets were sitting there on the ground, along with the plastic in which the cases had been shrink-wrapped. The driver picked up the plastic and tried to give it to me.

I said, "I don't want that." He was trying to stick me with disposing of his trash, and he had an empty truck to haul it away.

He said, "Well, you're gonna *do* something, aren't you?" Whatever that meant!

I said, "No, I'm not going to *do* anything with it. You keep the plastic."

He actually refused to take it. He dumped the plastic on the ground, gave me a dirty look, got back in the truck, and tore off. I couldn't believe it.

☑ What Should Be Done?

First of all, I should not have had to call the company and ask why they were late. Instead they should have been proactive and called me to say, "We are running a little bit late. Is there anything we can do for you in the meantime?"

Then, when I told them I was paying people extra money to wait for a truck that was hours late, the company could have said, "Well, if you can just show us some sort of documentation, we would be happy to deduct that from your bill because we want to do business with you again."

The bottom line is that this company is probably run by a moron or by an unbalanced person who constantly beats up on his people. Every employee is negative and has a bad attitude.

These people could learn how to provide good customer service if they received a little positive motivation and training—and probably a dose of something to alter their body chemistry.

But that hasn't happened. These companies didn't care one bit. So I have never called the same company again if I could help it.

OUTTA DETROIT AUTOMOBILE MANUFACTURER AND DEALERSHIP

My friend Brad London owns Assured Car Rental in Cleveland. While I was with him in his office, he got a phone call from a customer who had rented a 1995 automobile to go to Vermont and go skiing. Before he got to the ski resort, the car broke down in a little town in Vermont. He went to the local new-car dealer.

The dealer said, "No problem. We can get the part for you, but we can't get it until Monday."

This is Friday. Do these people really have to hang around this town all weekend instead of skiing?

I suggested to Brad, "Why don't we call the dealer there and see if they can borrow the part from another car?"

Brad called the dealership, but the service manager there wouldn't do it. He would rather have Brad's customer wait until Monday.

Now this is Outta Detroit, an automobile manufacturer that talks about customer service, satisfaction, and so forth. All they had to do was take a working part out of one of their new cars, put it in Brad's car, and on Monday, when the parts came in, put the new part in the dealer's car. Both cars were under the new-car warranty, so there wouldn't be any problem with the billing, and it wouldn't hurt anyone.

"We can't do it," the Vermont dealer said.

Brad said, "This is a popular model. You must have it on your lot."

The dealer said, "Yeah, we have eight of these models on the lot."

Brad said, "You're not going to sell all eight of them today and tomorrow, not in January, not even if you were in a big city."

The dealer wouldn't budge. As if he was really afraid he might sell all eight cars in the next two days! This scenario is a perfect example of how large companies talk about customer service but don't do anything about it. This dealer had forgotten—if he ever knew—who his customer is.

Brad's customer had to rent another car, drive that car back home, and leave Brad's car in that town in Vermont. Assured

Car Rental had to go to the extra inconvenience and expense of paying someone to fly to Vermont and bring the car back. All this happened because a new-car dealer in Vermont didn't care about service.

The ironic part about this story is that it happened when this automobile manufacturer had all kinds of publicity about their future in *Automotive News* and on CNN and major networks. It involved eliminating some of the dealers, getting dealers to cooperate, and basically trying to get everyone to want to buy their cars or trucks.

Many automobile manufacturers use car-rental companies to introduce prospective owners to their cars. If a car-rental customer really likes the rental car, then maybe he or she will want to buy one.

The amazing part about this story is that the Vermont dealership did everything possible to make things difficult and unpleasant for Assured's customer.

Obviously, the dealership was not going to sell every single one of the eight cars sitting in the showroom. And the auto part needed could have come in over the weekend, with lots of time to spare. What this service manager was saying, in words and actions, was that he was going to be totally uncooperative with a prospective buyer.

Because of this experience, Assured's customer and his party will never want to drive this car again. Why should they want to buy this brand of car? Why should they buy a car from anybody with that dealer's attitude? They will be sour toward this manufacturer forever.

☑ What Should Be Done?

Before we look at what should have been done, we must look at this industry. In most cases, the automobile manufacturer and the dealer are not true partners, in fact, the relationship of-

25

ten appears to be an adversarial one. It seems that car dealers are always fighting with the manufacturers or complaining about them. (Later in this book, you'll learn that Saturn and Lexus take a very different approach.)

Since there is virtually no monitoring of dealerships, the dealer can cause poor customer relations. He can hurt the customer and can prevent the manufacturer from selling more cars to that dissatisfied customer.

This situation was so easy to rectify, but here's an example in which saying "no" was just easier than saying "yes"—no long-term thinking, no looking at the big picture.

The dealer should have said, "No problem. All we have to do is to remove a part from one of our cars. It will take 45 minutes, and there's no charge. You are driving a car that's covered by the manufacturer's warranty, and we want you to be happy driving it. Can we get you some coffee? Do you want to go across the street and shop while we switch the part?"

That approach would have made Assured's customer and party feel very special and important. And then they would have told people for years, "That dealership in Vermont was great. *And Outta Detroit Automobile Manufacturer is great.*"

But again, there was no team playing, no common sense, no proper management.

LOST BAGGAGE AIRLINES

Vacations are supposed to be fun. Hawaii is supposed to be paradise. Flying is supposed to be at least one step above Greyhound (and at least two steps above if you fly first-class).

So why is flying becoming more of a hassle each year? And why is it so unpleasant? (And why do I always get stuck sitting next to someone who never learned how to dress in public, like the guy with his undershirt and his tattoos showing?)

I left for Hawaii flying Continental Airlines from Cleveland to Los Angeles to Honolulu. When my Continental flight to Hawaii was canceled, I got on Hawaiian Air, flew to Honolulu, and then flew to Maui on Lost Baggage Airlines. I got to Maui on Sunday at 4:00 P.M. only to discover that my luggage wasn't there. Everything was missing: my box of books, tapes, and materials for my seminar at the Maui Marriott—*and* my golf clubs, which I had brought so I could play a round of golf on Maui. I *did* have my personal luggage, the $189 carry-on I had bought—remember the first story in this chapter?—with the wheels that were still rolling.

Maui has a small airport, with just two luggage carousels. I went to baggage services, near the carousels, to tell them my luggage was lost.

The woman at the counter said, "No problem, we'll find it." She was really sweet.

That was around 5:00 P.M. At 9:00 P.M. they still hadn't found my luggage, and they had no idea where it was.

I had a gorgeous suite overlooking the ocean. I went to bed but I couldn't sleep. My body hadn't adjusted to the time change. So at 3:30 A.M., which is 9:30 A.M. Cleveland time, I got up, took the phone onto the balcony, and started making calls to Linda, who is my office manager and the person in charge of keeping me in line.

I thought, "This is one of the smarter things I have done in my life. Rather than get aggravated and go crazy, I will try to improve a bad situation." There I was, on the balcony of this gorgeous hotel suite in Maui, without my seminar materials—and without the golf clubs I dragged with me all the way from Cleveland just so I could play one round of golf on Maui.

Linda helped me try to track down my luggage back on the mainland, which is what people in Hawaii call our part of the world between Canada and Mexico. I wasn't getting anywhere being nice, so I had to get mean and yell at people, but at least I could have a beautiful sunrise and an unbelievable environment. So it was a kind of game, and I wasn't getting mad at myself.

Soon I was watching a gorgeous sunrise, still making calls. We worked our way west across the continent. We started in New York—after all, it was light there, and who knows? my stuff could have been there. We called everywhere we could think of, mostly Continental, because my flight originated with them. We called Cleveland, Houston, everywhere. A full day later, they still had no idea where my luggage was. None. No response.

The frustrating thing was that, besides losing my materials for the program, I had lost half a day, the only time I had set aside to play golf. And on Monday, every time I called Lost Baggage Airlines, I got the same answer: nothing, nothing, nothing.

They kept saying, "We'll find your luggage."

Monday evening around 8:00 I returned to the hotel and got a message. Someone from Lost Baggage Airlines, a guy named Robert, had called at noon and said, "We found your luggage. It will be your hotel at 1:00 P.M." That meant my luggage should have been waiting for me when I got the message!

Tuesday evening I happened to walk into the hotel just as my publisher, Roger Herman, arrived. He was going to speak at the same seminar. He grabbed my arm and said, "Hal, have I got a surprise for you! Come with me."

He took me to his car, opened the trunk, and said, "I found this box at the airport, lying a few feet away from the carousel."

There was my box of books, with my name plastered all over the box!

I said, "Did you find any golf clubs?"

He hadn't.

I couldn't believe that my box would be just sitting on the ground near the carousel all those hours after this guy Robert had said it would be at my hotel!

I got on the phone to Lost Baggage Airlines and asked for a supervisor and read her the riot act. I hated to be mean, but I went so crazy that they found my golf clubs and put them in a taxicab, which got to my hotel 35 minutes later that evening.

They arrived more than 48 hours after all this started. It's another customer service story about people who really care, or who say they do.

I still find it incredible that my publisher, who happened to be speaking at the same seminar with me, should literally stumble across my luggage at the airport and bring my box in his car after someone from the airlines had left me a message a day and a half earlier saying they had found my luggage and would have it delivered right away to my hotel.

I had to go crazy to get my golf clubs delivered.

☑️ What Should Be Done?

For one thing, Lost Baggage Airlines should have used a commonsense approach. They should have said, "Sir, we are so sorry this has happened. Can you please tell us your agenda so that we can accommodate you in any way we can." They should have asked, "What are your plans for the next 24 hours?"

Then I could have said, "Well, I planned to play a round of golf when I got to Hawaii."

They could then have said, "There's no problem. Where will you be playing and when? If we find the clubs before then, we can deliver them to the golf course. If we can't get your clubs there in time and you have to rent clubs, send us the bill, and we will reimburse you."

The 5th Wave

By Rich Tennant

"I THINK IT'S GOING TO TAKE MORE THAN FREE PEANUTS TO KEEP THE PASSENGERS HAPPY AFTER THIS ONE, SIR."

©The 5th Wave by Rich Tennant, Rockport, MA. E-mail: the5wave@tiac.net.

The airline could have tried anything to accommodate me. But instead, I had to sit by the phone, like a teenager waiting for a date, waiting for the airline to call. This waiting makes a person anxious and nervous, which makes the situation even worse.

Everything turned out all right in the end, but it was no way to take care of a customer. Would I ever want to fly Lost Baggage Airlines again? Not if I could help it. If I did have to fly with them, would I be nervous about checking any luggage on their plane? Of course.

The least they should have done in this case was avoid complete stupidity.

Oh yeah, I played a round of golf on Hawaii, but I had to rent clubs.

Postscript

A year later, I returned to Maui to speak. To get to Maui, I had to take Lost Baggage Airlines from Honolulu. Guess what? Lost Baggage Airlines lost my luggage again. But this airline is improving. My books arrived on the next flight, several hours later.

Lost Baggage Airlines didn't lose my golf clubs, though, because this time I was smart. I left my clubs at home.

3 Discount Heaven and Hell

HOME BUILDERS NIGHTMARE STORE

Who is running the asylum—the guards or the inmates? What kind of training is there? Is the policy: "Let's aggravate as many customers as we can and see how much they will take before they break down"?

Most home-repair discount stores are known for poor service (see the cartoon). We all know it, and we accept it. The blame rests on us . . . and we still accept more poor service.

Competition is healthy. The more, the better, and the better the companies are, the better the industry becomes. If we put our foot down and demand better service, we will get it. If we don't demand it, we will continue to be treated poorly. Enough said from my soapbox. It's time for another day in customer-service hell.

First, let me say that the day before this episode, I went to Home Builders Nightmare, spent $100, and had no problems. I went back the next day because I needed six pieces of rebar. The shelf tag said they cost 45 cents each.

The checkout lines were long. I stood there with $3 in one hand and the rebars in the other. After waiting in line forever, I got to the cashier. At this magic moment, the store decided to change cashiers, so now I had to wait again. The cashiers counted all the money in the drawer while I stood there, watching them. It was more important for them to count the money than it was to take care of a customer.

Finally, the cashier was ready. She didn't smile at me. She didn't even look at me. Nothing. She picked up a rebar and said, "I don't know the price."

I said, "They're marked 45 cents each."

She said, "Well, I have to go check," and she went to the customer service counter, which was right next to me.

I waited five minutes, watching her going through books. Being nice and helpful, I called over to her, "For whatever it's worth, they're 45 cents each. I don't know if that will help you."

Another employee was standing there at the customer service counter. I don't know what his job was, but he was wearing a tie, so I figured he must have been some kind of supervisor.

He yelled over to me, "Not a chance." He actually said that in front of everyone, and with customers behind me.

So I said, "Wait. Are you telling me there's not a chance these rebars are 45 cents each?"

He said, "That's correct."

I said, "So therefore, you are calling me a liar."

He said, "I didn't say that."

I said, "Yes, you did. *Not a chance* is saying that I'm making this up or that I'm lying."

He said, "I didn't say that."

I said, "Well, any court of law would assume that's the same thing as calling me a liar. I demand an apology."

Well, he gave me a look like, "Not in this lifetime." Not until dinosaurs come back and take over the earth.

In the meantime, the cashier found the price and returned to the register. Guess what. I was right. The rebars *did* cost 45 cents. Now her behavior was really hostile. She wouldn't look up at me. She wouldn't say thank you. By now I was really disgusted. I put my $3 back in my pocket and gave her a $100 bill so she had to make change and count it out for me.

I said, "Have a real nice day," and walked out.

Just for the heck of it, when I got home, I called the manager to let him know about the treatment I received. He said what managers always say in a situation like this. He said he said he would look into it. Somehow I really doubt it.

Obviously, this particular Home Builders Nightmare Store has terrible management from the top down because as soon as I had a little problem with the cashier, the manager—what-

©The 5th Wave by Rich Tennant, Rockport, MA. E-mail: the5wave@tiac.net.

ever his title—and the cashier banded together against me, the customer, rather than with me.

These people obviously never heard the motto, "The customer is always right." And they certainly never heard that "The customer is in charge."

☑ What Should Be Done?

This manager should never have argued with me and insulted me. He should have just said, "Sir, is that the price you believe it is? No problem." Or he could have said, "Can you hold on for just a second. We have to check."

What should have been obvious to everyone was that a lot of time and aggravation could have been avoided very simply.

Someone on the payroll of Home Builders Nightmare, should have thought, "This guy says rebars cost 45 cents apiece. So if I ask for an employee to go to that aisle and look at the shelf, I should get a confirmation of the price."

Instead, they took ten times as long, argued with me, and irritated me. Does all that make me want to return to Home Builders Nightmare? Not at all.

When another company comes in and sets up business right next to Home Builders Nightmare—a company like Home Depot, for example—the new store will find that attracting business is a piece of cake.

HOME BUILDERS NIGHTMARE STORE (AGAIN!)

Why do we run to the superstores? Are they really super? If they are, what makes them super? We know that in many cases it's not super employees. In many cases, it's perception. We think the price will be much cheaper. But is it really? and by how much?

Sometimes I think that we—myself included—are not educated consumers. And sometimes, if the price is cheaper, it may not be worth the aggravation involved. Should I have to wait in a long line to save $1? $2? Am I spending that much in gas money to get to the superstore? What are my real savings?

The small business is *not* dead! Many small companies are hanging on, waiting out the storm, ready to prove that small is better. Here's proof.

I needed a new disposal. I went to Home Builders Nightmare in spite of my earlier experience because they were the closest and most convenient, and I knew they would have a competitive price. I went to the plumbing area and saw two different models, one for $53 and one for $44.

Usually it's not easy to find an employee, but I finally found a guy.

I said, "Which one of these is better?"

He said, "Well, I think the more expensive one would be better."

I said, "Is there any reason why?"

He said, "Probably price." He obviously didn't know anything at all about the product. I got the more expensive one because I thought it might be a little better.

Now I had to get out of the store. The checkout area had four registers open with at least seven people in each line. It was so crowded that I just put the disposal down, left it, and walked out.

☑ What Should Be Done?

This company should do what Ace Hardware did. I went to Ace because it also was near my home. I thought, "I will spend more money, but it will be a convenient location."

The disposal actually cost $9 less, about $44. The clerk explained to me that one company manufactures most of the disposals sold, and that the one at Ace was made by the same manufacturer as the disposal I found at Home Builders Nightmare but with a different private label. I was taken care of at Ace in one-two-three order. The guy also explained a few things about the disposal unit so it could be installed easily.

This experience just goes to show how one person can make a difference and that a smaller store takes care of their customers properly.

By the way, there was no one in line when I checked out. Easy. So I can't tell you much about their customer service at the cash register. Maybe I just got lucky!

OVERMEDICATE YOU DRUG STORES

I **was driving along when I thought, "Wow! I need some gum and dental floss."** I saw Overmedicate You, one in a large chain of discount drug stores. I zoomed into a parking space and zipped into the store. (You can tell by now that I am a Type A.) I found what I needed in two minutes flat and took it to the checkout.

One line was open. There was only one person ahead of me, but I could tell it wasn't going to be quick. The cashier was looking for the customer's film, and already I had stood in line longer than the time it had taken me to come in, find my stuff, and take it to the register.

Another employee was just a few feet away from me. He was crouching down on the floor, cutting open boxes of windshield-washer fluid.

In my most polite Mr. Nice voice, I said, "Sir, is it possible that you could open up another line?"

He said, "Sir, you are the next in line, and she will take care of you soon."

His attitude was real snippy. In fact, he was downright rude. I was embarrassed that he talked to me this way in front of other people. Nobody deserves to be talked to this way in front of other people.

So I said, "Can you please get up and come here so I can talk to you." When I could see him face to face, I said, "I might work for Overmedicate You or I might not, but either way, I am going to make sure that today is your last day, because I am going to call Overmedicate You and complain."

Well, when I called the corporate office and told them exactly what happened and how their employee talked to me, they said, "Well, sometimes that's the way it is." Amazing! Is that any kind of answer to give a customer?

☑ What Should Be Done?

First, as I mentioned before, the employee should never have talked to me that way, and certainly not in front of other people. Second, the corporate office should never have told me that what happened was business as usual. I couldn't believe I was being treated a second time like that!

They should have said, "Sir, we are so sorry you had that experience. We want to make it up to you. What's your address? We are going to send you a gift certificate."

If they said that and spent $5 on a gift certificate, it would guarantee that I would return to their store. They just don't care. You can tell by the way they operate their stores.

This experience is a perfect example of the trickle-down effect. When we examine the world's best companies later in this book, you will find that salary or job title is not necessarily what determines great customer service. As I have mentioned before and will say over and over again, great service starts at the top.

Think about how much fun it is to work for someone you respect and maybe even like. You enjoy pleasing this person, which you do by performing your job well. I believe we all have had jobs where we loved our boss and jobs where we wished the boss would turn into a hamster.

Treat your employees with respect, kindness, and empathy. Do that, and (in most cases) your employees will do the same for your customers. I say this in response to the cynics and critics who say, "Hey, it's just a minimum-wage job. What can you expect?" I'm sure we can all think of places that pay just a few bucks per hour where we were pleased with the service and also received a warm smile.

BRAIN DEAD ELECTRONICS STORE

People ask me, "Which is your favorite horror story?" This one definitely has to be one of the top five contenders.

I don't know if you have ever read *Mad* magazine (or if you are lucky enough to be able to remember it). This great magazine ran a cartoon called "*Mad*'s Snappy Answers to Those Stupid Questions." This cartoon supplied those quick answers we all wish we could think of on the spot instead of an hour or a day later.

Well, in this case, I got lucky. I actually thought of a snappy comeback. I decided not to get mad, but to get even. And whatever you think of me (I am not an evil guy, really), it was fun. I could imagine the expression on this clerk's face when her boss informed her that I was *not* who I said I was. And then I could imagine her boss asking her, "What is this all about?" She would have to say something about what she did and backpedal herself out of the situation.

Great customer service is not an accident. It takes thought, planning, and of course the right players to make a winning team.

Brain Dead sells electronics and miscellaneous stuff. I went in, got the new Steely Dan Live CD, and took it to the check-out counter. The clerk's name was Tiffany, and I don't know when I saw anyone move more slowly. And she was talking to her buddy. Tiffany and her buddy weren't really ignoring me, but I definitely got the impression that I was more of a nuisance than a customer.

I said, "Excuse me, I'm kind of in a hurry. Will you be able to ring me up?" So now, Tiffany decided to ring my sale up very, very s-l-o-w-l-y. All the while she kept talking with her buddy.

I said, "Excuse me, I'm really in a hurry. Can you cut your conversation, and do it a little bit later? I don't mind if you talk, but why don't you do it as soon as I leave."

I could see the cash register drawer, which was open right in front of me. I saw every quarter, dime, nickel, and penny. Instead of giving me the loose ones, she decided to break open every new roll of coins so that she could go even s-l-o-w-e-r.

Now, I thought, "It's time to mess back with her." So, just as she finished, I said, "What's your name?" I looked at her name badge. I said, "Tiffany, hi. My name is Jon Lief [my friend Jon and I always use each other's names in situations like this]. That's Mr. L-i-e-f, and I want you to know that I am from corporate. I am from the shopper's program, and you have been shopped, which means that your customer service was atrocious.

"I want you to go to your manager as soon as I walk out and tell him Mr. Lief was here from corporate. Let him know that today is your last day. Because as soon as I get in my car, I am writing up a report, and I'm faxing it to the home office to explain why you will no longer be working for Brain Dead. You will not represent our corporation any longer. Tiffany, have a really good day."

And I walked out. You should have seen the look on her face. Can you imagine her going to her boss and mentioning Mr. Lief, and her boss saying, "Who? We don't have a corporate shopper's program. There's no Mr. Lief."

I ruined her day.

☑️ What Should Be Done?

The answer is very simple. This person should go work at the bureau of motor vehicles, where employees can be as slow and as nasty as they want because they have a job for life.

A person like this should be let go. This attitude is totally inexcusable.

The managers need to get out of their offices and on the floor more often so they can observe their employees.

Actually, it goes back even farther than that: to the hiring policy. This episode is another case of management hiring the wrong person just to put a lukewarm body in a spot rather than looking for someone who has the right attitude, someone who can represent the company and create the desired image.

4 Gizmos and Glitches

COMPUTER HELL #1
AND COMPUTER HELL #2

First, let me say that Computer Hell #1–a computer super-store–is another company that has gone out of business. I was buying a computer for my business, and I wanted to buy an integrated software package called Claris Works. I wanted to install a huge database—at least to me it was huge—of 3,500 names.

First I went to Hell #1 and asked a salesperson my questions. One thing I especially wanted to know was exactly how many names this database could hold.

The salesperson said, "A couple hundred."

Next I went to Hell #2. There the salesperson said, "Five hundred."

That really got me going. Literally. I decided to go back to both stores, and I purposely went at a different time and made a point of asking a different person. I figured the answer would be 200 or 500, and that would settle the matter.

This time a salesperson at Hell #1 said, "One thousand."

That was *not* what I had expected!

When I went back to Hell #2 the clerk's answer this time was, "Ten thousand."

Incredible! Nobody had any idea—and neither did I!

☑ What Should Be Done?

The solution is so simple. All they had to do was to get my name and phone number, to call the company that manufactures the product, ask for technical support, get an answer for me, call me back, and then sell me the package.

Every time I think of this story, a flashback occurs to a great skit on *Saturday Night Live* in the late 1980s. In this skit, called "The Liar," Jon Lovitz played a character who was incapable of telling the truth. He just made up stuff on the spot.

I can just hear Jon Lovitz saying, "Yeah, 10,000, that's it. This database will hold 10,000 names. It's huge. In fact, maybe it will hold even 10 *million* names. Yeah, it will hold the names of all the people in Asia. . . . That's the ticket!"

Boy, am I tired of people just making stuff up. I am *so* impressed when someone says, "I don't know, but I'll find out." It's so rare when people offer to do more than is expected of them and then actually follow up.

It's really so simple. If I had wanted them to make something up, I would have asked for the Fiction Department.

COULD BE BETTER APPLIANCES

Sometimes I wish a camera crew could just follow me around **for a day.** Even better, I wish I had one of those secret cameras in my briefcase, they way they do on television shows like *20/20*.

I wonder whether some people are born stupid, or do they get that way? Maybe there's something in our appliances or our air conditioning systems that seeps into salespeople's brains.

Either way, this experience caused me to start shaking my head as soon as I hung up the phone. I couldn't believe what the salesperson had told me over the phone. The only thing even more unbelievable was what happened afterward in the store. By the way, Could be Better is also out of business.

My refrigerator died just when I was about to sell my old house. Great. Just what I wanted to do—sink more money into a house I was trying to sell.

I should have realized there would be problems when I walked in to this appliance retailer and saw the salespeople wearing polyester suits—one step up from leisure suits. But I saw a refrigerator that was okay, and I ordered it.

When the refrigerator was delivered, it had two holes on the front panel where the brand name was supposed to be. So I called Could be Better.

They said, "That's the way they come, with no name plate."

I thought, "You have got to be kidding me. No way."

I had to go back to the store. I saw the same type of refrigerator, and of course, just as I remembered, it had a nameplate on it.

So I told the salesperson, "Your guys delivered one of these without a nameplate, so I want you to pick up the refrigerator you just delivered or else watch me while I steal a nameplate off this refrigerator."

☑ What Should Be Done?

They should have said on the phone, "Sir, we are so sorry. We have a nameplate for you. Is it possible for you to come in, or do you want us to mail you one?" That's all they had to do.

Deep in my heart, I know this episode is why they are out of business. Well, okay, this episode is one of a thousand reasons why.

The scary part of this story is that I *had* to go back to the store and actually take a nameplate off a refrigerator that was a floor model while the salesperson watched.

CLUELESS IN PRODUCT KNOWLEDGE
ELECTRONICS SUPERSTORE

couldn't wait to get into this place. An electronics superstore is my kind of candy shop, and I'd heard that the Clueless in

Product Knowledge Electronics Superstore was owned by a huge corporation and was one of a few places in the United States where you could get tremendous help and knowledge on every electronic gizmo known to humankind.

I went there to look at televisions. They must have had 100 different models. One aisle had models with screens 25 to 27 inches, another aisle had models with screens 30 to 32 inches, and so on. In the 25- to 27-inch aisle I saw two RCA sets, one on the right and the other on the left.

Both had the same front, same cabinet, same everything. I looked and looked at them, but the only difference I could see was that one had "SEQ stereo" in the upper left corner of the cabinet, and the other had "SEQ stereo" in the upper *right* corner. What puzzled me was that one set was marked $298 and the other was $348.

I even looked at the back of the sets for manufacturing dates. If one of the models was newer, it could cost more. But both sets were made during the same month and year.

So I asked the salesperson, "Excuse me, can you explain to me the difference between these two?"

He said, "Price." He obviously had no idea.

I said, "Thank you so much for helping me." He actually thought he had helped me—he *really was* totally clueless.

I asked another salesperson. She had no idea, either. Then she started making stuff up.

She said, "Well, you know, with some televisions we're not sure, so we match the price, so if it's a lower price we might match it."

I had no idea what she meant, but I got the message. She too was clueless. She obviously had no idea if there was any difference between the two or why the prices were different. I went into the VCR section to see if anyone there could help me with televisions. I couldn't find anyone who could help or who had any idea of what was going on.

The last I heard, the huge corporation that owned Clueless in Product Knowledge was closing these stores.

☑ What Should Be Done?

In my opinion, the reason for this experience rests with management. Of course, given the wages and the sheer volume of the product line and the speed with which new products come onto the market, it is almost impossible for some of the salespeople to learn every product in the area. But the best people will learn all that they can because they have a passion for electronics or for the industry.

So, the first thing management should do is to have updates and quizzes on product knowledge. But as you know, the retail business offers virtually no training whatsoever on sales skills or even common sense.

If we as managers make product knowledge an important part of the job, then it will be. We have to follow up with quizzes and different types of training.

Telling someone to do something doesn't guarantee that it will be done. Imagine bringing home a six-week-old puppy, opening the back door, and saying, "Go . . . and come back when you're done." Or imagine that you look at your fully housebroken dog and decide that you're tired of going out into the rain and the snow and the dark, that you want your paper delivered to your favorite chair. You can't just hold the door open and say, "Woofer, be a good fellow and bring me the paper when you come back in."

People also need additional training. The more we do something and get helpful feedback, the better we become at the task at hand.

In my situation the salesperson should have said one of two things: either, "I don't know. Let me find out," or "Do you want to come with me while I find out? Or you can wait here, and I will be right back."

Ideally, of course, the salespeople should have taken some time to learn the product before I came in. Either way, they would have had an intelligent answer when I asked about the difference between the two television sets.

The thing they should *not* have done was to make something up. To this date, I still have no idea what the difference was between the two sets.

Nor did I buy.

SUPER NOVA APPLIANCES

Now, I can understand that companies have certain policies because those policies make sense. Some percentage of the public might buy a camcorder or similar product, go on vacation, use the product, and then try to return it for a full refund. But this situation happens very rarely.

Some policies are stupid. If you have ever tried on clothes in a discount department store, you probably have seen the sign, "Only three garments allowed at a time in fitting rooms." Why is the sign there? Are two out of every three customers potential shoplifters?

The fact is that, on the average, only a very small percentage of customers shoplift—the problem is mostly internal, with employees the culprits. So the sign is telling 98% of the customers, "We don't trust you" and "We're going to inconvenience you."

In short, certain policies should really be thought out before they are implemented. In fact management should ask itself, "Is this policy good for us, our customers, or both?" The best companies satisfy both!

By the way, I think by the time you read this book, Super Nova will be out of business or will be having financial problems.

I wanted to buy a big-screen television with rear projection. Now, Super Nova had a number of stores around town, and I figured some were bigger than others. I went to the store nearest to me and walked up to the first salespeople I saw, two guys standing together and talking to each other.

I said, "Is your inventory here different from what they have at your other stores?"

One guy turned to me and said, "What are you doing? Playing us against each other for a better price?"

I said something that can't be repeated here. Then I said, "Don't just assume that. I came to this store because it's closer. I just want to know if you have different inventory at different stores."

Well, Super Nova had the television I wanted, so I decided to buy it there, even though these salespeople sure didn't know much.

Now, all my other television sets had a standard picture tube. Rear projection was new to me.

So I told the salesperson, "I have a problem. I have a lot of windows behind me, and I have never had rear projection. I would like to make sure that I don't get glare on the screen and that the picture isn't too light. If this rear projection doesn't work well because of the setup in my home, can I return the set and just get my money back? It will only take me five minutes to test and see if I have trouble with rear projection. In fact, if it doesn't work in my house, I will even pay for delivering the set back to your store."

The salesperson said, "No, we don't do that."

I said, "What do you do?"

He said, "If you take the set and it doesn't work, we just give you a due bill."

I said, "No. I just want to try it."

So I got the manager. He confirmed what the salesperson had told me.

I said, "Do you mean you *don't* do it or that you *won't* do it?"

He said, "No."

I couldn't believe it. Super Nova wouldn't even let a customer try something like this. It wasn't as if I wanted to take one of their camcorders on vacation and return it after I came back from the trip. I just wanted to see if the product would work in my home.

☑ What Should Be Done?

Super Nova should have done what Sears department stores do. I went to Sears.

Sears said, "We have a 30-day return policy." They couldn't have been nicer. They had the identical television set, and it was the same price, to the penny.

I had never bought any electronics at Sears. I said, "I only need a few minutes to try it."

They said, "Oh, don't worry. You have 30 days."

So guess where I bought my rear-projection television set. At Sears. It worked out just great. In fact, since then I have bought a second, upgraded model. Guess where I got it.

5 Room Service

"HAL" BERLY

My friend and mentor Bob Shook, who is a big-time author, says that a person who copies one person's stuff plagiarizes, but that a person who copies 50 people's stuff is doing research. I was going to say that I have made a career of plagiarizing, but on second thought, you could say that I am a great researcher.

I have very few original ideas. So I have copied others. But I have always copied the best.

It is much easier to improve the wheel than to reinvent it. So it blows me away to think how many people try to reinvent the wheel when we already have so many perfectly fine wheels out there.

All hotels do pretty much the same thing, and it's pretty basic: rooms for sleeping, rooms for meetings, and rooms for eating and drinking. To provide and maintain all these rooms, hotels have sales staff, catering staff, housekeeping staff, and so on.

Why not copy from the best in your business? They charge more and keep their customers happy. This principle can be applied to the Ritz-Carlton as well as to Night-eze Motel. It's a matter of taking the time to observe and study, and then proceeding to copy, copy, copy.

What made my experience at this hotel so amazing is that the "Hal" Berly is classified as a fine hotel. I checked in as a speaker. Now, when I do this, the organization that is bringing me in pays for the hotel. The bill is put on the organization's standing account or on its credit card.

Often when I check in, the hotel staff will say, "Now, this account covers only the room and the tax, so we would like your credit card to cover everything else—meals, gift shop, and telephone."

I *never* give them a credit card because I find it much easier if I pay cash for things like meals and incidental purchases. And the phone calls, which usually add up to $2 or $3, are generally billed to the organization that is sponsoring the seminar.

I pay cash because it speeds up the checkout process. Besides, things can get messed up so easily, and then it's *my* pain in the neck to get them straightened out. So I pay cash for everything when I stay at a hotel.

Well, this clerk at the registration desk at "Hal" Berly insisted on taking my credit card for phone calls.

I said, "No, I'm making only three credit-card calls, and I don't want to go through the checkout precedure for a couple bucks."

Finally, the clerk said okay, it was no problem. But when I went to make an outside call from the phone in my room, all I got was that *whee-a-whee* whine. They hadn't turned my phone on.

I had to call the front desk twice to have my phone turned on. They did turn it on, but a couple hours later, I discovered they had turned it off again. I had to call to get the phone turned back on.

The next morning, the phone was turned off again. I had to call the manager at the front desk to get my phone turned on. It took two calls, but I got it.

And the next morning—you guessed it—the phone was turned off again. In case you're not counting, this is my fourth attempt and eighth call. I was furious. The phone was turned back on.

I did have something else to do besides call the management about the phone in my room. I really *do* have a life. I was at the hotel for a seminar and luncheon for an advertising association.

While I was in the middle of presenting the seminar, an employee walked up to me and handed me a bill for the meeting room and luncheon. He wanted me to sign it.

I said, "I'm just the speaker, I'm not the one who signs for it. That's for the association to do, and there's nobody here who can sign it."

He said, "Well, I'll just leave it on the table."

I said, "What? Is God going to pick it up then? Attach it to the master account!" Here I was, telling this guy what to do, and this is supposed to be a fancy hotel.

When I went to check out, they wanted me to pay for the phone calls. Not the same old hassle again! I told them something I'd never say to my grandmother.

This is supposed to be a fine hotel. Yeah.

☑ What Should Be Done?

They should have made a note in the computer that I would not use a credit card but that the phone should be kept on. That's it. Simple!

But here, technology and stupidity got the upper hand. This hotel had a poor system and clueless management. Their people only knew how to say no. They couldn't think out of the box or take the initiative. They certainly didn't put the customer first.

So whether I went up the ladder or down the ladder, the system still did not work. It seems that nobody communicated my request to anyone on the night shift or the next day's shift. And so I kept having problems.

The other problem, the employee who tried to leave the bill with me, is another classic example of "It's not my job" and a lack of communication.

When I go into a place like this, I always have the feeling that their people are sent to "No-I-can't" seminars instead of "Yes-I-can" seminars.

This hotel should take a page from Ritz-Carlton, where they say, "Any employee who receives a guest complaint owns the complaint." Each person should be responsible for his or her area and should be able to take care of the problem.

You *can* teach employees to be accountable. It's done with three little words: training, training, training.

"HAL" TON

The logical way to look at this situation is to understand that hardly any hotel chain owns the hotels that bear its name. The hotels are run by management companies that own anywhere from one property to dozens or hundreds of hotels. The keys to success are the people each hotel hires, how those people are trained, and whether that hotel takes advantage of the resources offered by the hotel chain.

Hotels are pretty much like McDonald's—there are great ones, and once in a while you come across one that could use improvement. So I can't blame the entire chain for a poor management team at one location, even though I would like to.

Ideally, for the hotel chain and its customers, each hotel's staff is always trying to outdo all the other hotels. This way, the whole chain or industry rises to a better level of customer service.

* * * *

Here I was at another fine hotel. At 8:00 P.M. or so, I called the front desk and asked for an iron and ironing board. A voice said, "We are all out of ironing boards."

I said, "I really need an iron. I'm the speaker at a meeting tomorrow morning."

At 9:30 P.M. I still had no ironing board, so I called again. And again at 10:00 P.M., and yet again, my fourth phone call, at 10:30 P.M.

I said, "Look, I *really* need an ironing board and an iron."

The voice said, "I'm sorry, we have 30 irons, but they are all gone."

I said, "Look, I know how the hotel system works. What you can do, rather than just waiting until morning, is to spend a few minutes helping me. Go knock on some of the 30 doors of the guests who have those 30 irons, and find someone who's done with the iron. I promise you that all these people aren't ironing together in some kind of an ironing conference."

The voice said, "It's too late to do that."

I said, "You don't understand. Here's the deal. I've called four times, and I've waited two and a half hours. I can't be nice anymore. I am the speaker tomorrow for a meeting. If you want me to stand all wrinkled and disheveled in front of 400 people and tell them *why* I look this way, that it's because you didn't get me an iron, well, that's going to be your problem.

"I will mention names, and I will make sure I include the general manager of the hotel. I've been patient, I've been nice, but enough is enough. I suggest you go knock on some doors and get me an iron!"

Well, about five minutes later, the phone rang. It rang about six times. I had no desire to answer the phone, because I knew it was going to be another runaround. After all, if they had my iron, they would have been knocking at my door, not calling me on the phone.

But I did answer the phone, and it *was* another runaround. In fact, the voice even said, "Well, if you want, you can talk to my night manager."

I said, "I don't want to talk to your night manager. I don't want you to pass the buck. I want you to get me an iron." And I unplugged the phone.

Well, what I really did was to rip it out of the wall. I felt as if I were in a movie. Besides, I carry spare phone cords.

A guy came to the door, a young kid, a real nice kid named Chris. I said, "Look Chris, I'm not kidding around. I can't go downstairs tomorrow and get up in front of all these people looking wrinkled like a bulldog. I'm an author—in fact, I'll even prove it to you. Here's my book."

He looked at my picture on the cover and said, "That's *you*." Suddenly I had a new fan, who was saying how he read my book and how it changed his life or something. He said, "I'll go to the Wal-Mart store and buy you an iron."

I said, "That's not necessary. Go knock on some doors."

Well, miraculously, about five minutes later, the house-keeper came up with an iron.

She said, "I went down to my car and got my own iron."

I said, "Thank you so much. I only need it for five minutes."

And that, I thought, is what it takes to get an iron and ironing board at the "Hal" Ton. Unbelievable.

☑ What Should Be Done?

This situation is a matter of people who just don't want to be helpful. I finally got a couple people who had the right attitude, a "yes, I can do it" attitude.

The key is for management to hire people with the right attitude. It's much easier to hire the right people and set them loose providing customer service than than it is to hire people with the wrong attitude and then spend the rest of your life trying—without success—to get them to change their ways.

Imagine how great this hotel, or any business, could be if everyone in the company had a "yes, I can" instead of a "no, I can't" attitude. The hotel staff had only to start calling the 30 rooms that had an iron and ask, "Are you done with your iron? Another guest needs one." They could have found a free iron in four or five calls. It was obvious that nobody wanted to spend the little bit of effort necessary to get me an iron.

This company is the kind in which somebody in management gets the idea that everybody should wear a button saying, "yes I can," but nobody has the attitude to match. Again, it's a matter of simple training and of positive customer service attitudes trickling from the top down. The members of the housekeeping staff—and probably other departments—need to be taught what they can do to satisfy the customer.

When you the customer deal with this type of company, you need to save your breath and your energy. Cut to the chase immediately and say, "Can I speak with the manager?" You don't want to talk to subordinates.

This scenario is a perfect example of no communication, no trickle-down effect. Only the managers are trained; nobody else has any authority or can do anything but stand there and go by policy.

To correct this situation, this company needs to use role-playing to simulate typical situations. Management needs to say, "What would you do in this situation?" Then when that situation or one like it happens in real life, the employee has the experience and knows what to do.

Seldom have I seen such inattention from almost an entire crew of subordinates; only one person had the training and the right attitudes to take care of me. It would be nice, by the way, for the management to call Chris's parents and commend them on doing a good job of raising their son.

This situation can be attributed to the manager. It can be rectified, but it will take time.

The 5th Wave
By Rich Tennant

"OH, I'LL GET US IN – I USED TO MANAGE THE FRONT DESK
AT A LARGE HOTEL CHAIN."

©*The 5th Wave by Rich Tennant, Rockport, MA. E-mail: the5wave@tiac.net.*

"I'm Sorry. . ."

If you start a sentence with "I'm sorry," you can follow it up
with anything you want, no matter how outrageous. Notice
how these two little words make the most unpleasant and difficult situations seem matter-of-fact, even mundane:

"I'm sorry, we can't refund your money."

"I'm sorry, the last plane left five minutes ago."

"I'm sorry, we accidentally put your dog to sleep."

"I'm sorry, our bulldozer leveled the wrong building."

"HAL" SON

I'm thinking of sending to this hotel 100 buttons that say, "No, you can't."

When I got to this hotel, all the staff people were wearing little round buttons saying, "Yes, you can." That was their motto. Well, that was the motto they were wearing.

I wanted something spectacular and very difficult. I wanted to have breakfast in the restaurant. I know, I know, I'm asking for way too much, but sometimes customers are like that!

It was 10:15 A.M. when I walked into the restaurant. There was no sign posted or anything to indicate that today was different or special.

I said, "I would like breakfast."

I was told, "sir, you will have to order room service. Today is Mother's Day, and we have brunch only."

I couldn't believe it. Here I was, doing a seminar, staying in a room that cost $150 per night, and I was playing second fiddle to people who walked in off the street for brunch. The restaurant was open, they had to have orange juice and bread and eggs, but they wouldn't serve me breakfast?

☑ What Should Be Done?

It's time to explore the policy decision-making process again. Who came up with this idea? Was it the restaurant manager, or was it even the general manager of this hotel?

Whoever was responsible should have asked which guests are the important ones. Sure, *all* guests are important, but shouldn't the guest who has a room have priority over a person who has come in just for Sunday brunch? If I have paid for a room, the hotel should make every effort to accommodate me, and that certainly includes the right to eat my meals in the hotel.

Even if I have to sit in a roped-off section, or if I have to retreat to the bar to be served, I should be able to sit down to a meal. It's bad enough that I can't share Mother's Day with my mother. As far as I'm concerned, eating any meal in my hotel room is about one step up from being sent to bed without any supper.

The staff should have said, "Sir, I'm sorry, the restaurant is closed because we are preparing for our brunch. We can make an exception for you because you're a guest and you expect breakfast." Or they could have said, "Is it okay with you if we have room service deliver breakfast to your room?"

They should have offered something for the inconvenience, like not charging me or splitting the cost. So I ordered oatmeal in my room. Gee, that was fun.

This hotel should have said to me, "Sir, what would it take to accommodate you?"

"HAL" NAC

I checked in and got a really nice suite. When I got up in the morning and went to take a shower, there was no hot water. I ran the hot water tap for a full five minutes, but the water was only lukewarm. I got dressed. I went to the front desk and talked to the woman there. Her tag said she was the front desk manager.

I said, "I'm a little disappointed. I have a great room, but I have no hot water."

She said, "Did you turn the knob all the way to the left?"

This question is not a good sign. Does she think that I have never taken a shower before? Or does she think we're talking about a new concept?

I said, "Yes, I did."

She said, "Well, it should work."

I said, "Well, no, it didn't."

End of conversation. She didn't offer anything. She didn't even say "I'm sorry." Nothing. You may expect this lack of service from run-of-the-mill or inferior hotels. Not from a fine hotel. But then again, we all expect and deserve a certain level of service no matter what we pay. I've had hotter water at a fleabag motel.

☑ What Should be Done?

The hotel should have done one of two things. First, they should have offered a solution. "Sir, we are so sorry to hear about this. Would you like to take a shower in another room?"

If they couldn't think of a solution, or if I didn't like their idea, they should have asked me what *would* satisfy me. "Or is there anything else we can do for you? What would you suggest we do for you to correct the situation?"

All they had to do was ask. I might have said, "Could you take $10 off my room charge?" And they could have topped it off with humor: "How about a complimentary breakfast? We promise you the coffee will be really hot!"

But instead they gave me directions on how to use the faucet, as if I had never taken a shower in my life.

Obviously, this individual had not been trained to solve problems, and this individual was not empowered to solve problems. This lack of training is shortsighted, because we know that to live is to have to deal with problems, especially if you are stationed at the front desk of a hotel.

I have come to realize that what separates the exceptional hotels from the so-so and the miserable ones is how they respond when I tell them that I don't want to give them my credit card to cover extra incidentals.

It's funny, but as I wrote this "What should be done" section, I was sitting in another hotel in this chain, this time in North Carolina, and I had just gone through the irritating check-in ritual that I mentioned at the beginning of this chapter. And of course, I'm here to do a seminar on sales and customer service.

When I check in at certain hotel chains, as I explained, I *always* run into this problem. After I give them my name and address and all those details, the person in registration always says, "We need a credit card for imprint for incidentals and extra."

Then I say, "We both know that my room and tax have been taken care of. I will not order room service. I'm not going to watch a movie. The only thing I will do is use my phone card to call my house or office, and I don't want to put that grand total of a dollar or two on my credit card—you can put that on the master account, and you already have a credit card number for that.

"I have two reasons for not wanting to use my card. First of all, I don't want to wait in a checkout line for such a small amount. And second, hotels have a way of double-billing, charging both me and the organization that is paying my hotel bill. If I want to rectify the double billing, I will have to get out all my client's letters and paperwork to prove to the credit card company that I shouldn't be billed."

The bottom line is that I avoid a lot of hassles later on by insisting that the front desk charge that couple of bucks to the organization that has brought me in. Invariably, I get involved in a discussion that ends with the staff *having* to drag a manager into the issue, and all for a measly buck or two. I can't

say it strongly enough: LET THE PEOPLE AT THE DESK MAKE A SIMPLE
DECISION. EVERYBODY WILL BE HAPPIER.

"HAL" SUITES

This event is probably my absolute favorite just because it is
so unbelievable. In fact, I tell this story in many of my seminars on customer service.

My friends say that living nightmares are really good story
material—that later, when it's all over, we laugh and say how
funny it was. Well, I realized this experience was hysterically
funny even as it was happening, because it was just so weird.

* * * *

This episode is one of the wildest ever. I left Cleveland, Ohio,
to do a seminar in Myrtle Beach and then two seminars in Ft.
Lauderdale. I had arranged to spend a couple of extra days in
Ft. Lauderdale with my girlfriend, who was going to meet me
in Charlotte and go with me to Ft. Lauderdale.

When I finished in Myrtle Beach and got to the airport, I
was disappointed to learn that all the flights from Cleveland
had been canceled because of weather, so my girlfriend could-
n't get out until the next day. When I got to Charlotte, I called
my voice mail again. Guess what? Her grandfather died, and so
she wasn't coming in at all. Obviously, I was even more disappointed, and at the same time, I felt bad because I wanted to
talk to her to see what was going on and how she was coping.

I got to Ft. Lauderdale and picked up my rental car. It was
after 11 P.M. when I finally got to the hotel.

As I walked in, the belhop said, "I wouldn't go in there if I
were you."

I replied, "Okay," and gave him a strange look. I went in and walked up to the front desk.

"Hi, my name is Hal Becker," I said. "I would like to register."

The person at the front desk responded, "I am sorry, sir. We are overbooked. We are in an oversold situation. We are out of rooms."

I said, "I can appreciate that, but I am the speaker for the meeting. See that big banner over there—that huge banner about seven feet long and that big sign for the association? Well, I am the keynote speaker for that meeting."

"I'm sorry, we are all out of rooms."

All I could say was, "Get your manager."

The manager came out.

I said, "*Excuse* me, I think we have a problem here."

The manager said, "I am sorry. We are out of rooms."

So, I pulled out my letter of confirmation on the association letterhead.

"Look," I said. "This reservation was made more than seven months ago. Here is the confirmation number. You don't understand. I am the speaker, and you don't bump speakers. I am the one they came to see."

The manager replied, "I'm sorry, sir. We are all out of rooms."

Now I was angry. I had never encountered this situation in my entire life.

While this conversation was happening, I was thinking, "Okay, wait. Maybe my girlfriend can still come in, but I doubt it. Either way, the first three nights are paid for by the association, and I am going to extend my stay for another two nights for myself. Maybe I can turn a bad situation to a better one."

I said to the manager, "Okay, I'll make you a deal. I won't go ballistic. If you look at your computer, you will see I am booked for five nights. The first three nights are billed directly to the association. The last two nights I want complimentary.

Not only do I want them complimentary, I also do not want to pay so much as a quarter for any phone calls. If I want to rent a movie, I don't even want to give you a credit card. *And* when I check out, I want you to take care of *everything* for inconveniencing me."

"Calm down, sir. Calm down," the manager replied.

"Give me your business card," I said to him.

"Why?" he asked.

I said, "I want you to sign the back of it. In case you die, I want a written confirmation of this agreement." And I was thinking, "Well, this stay won't turn out all bad."

He said, "We'll put you up at another hotel on the beach."

I thought, "I don't mind staying by the beach for just one night."

Now I was feeling pretty good about the situation. I had just saved $400 or $500 on my room for the last two nights of my visit. It's hard to pay for hotel rooms when you travel on someone else's dime as much I do.

So I drove to this beach hotel. There was nowhere to park my car—and I mean *nowhere*. I parked in front of the front door. I could tell this place was a *dump*. All I could hear was head-banging music coming from the lobby bar. Lots of thumping and loud music. I thought, "Oh, great."

I went to the front desk and got my key. It was such a dump that I couldn't even get to my room by walking through the lobby. I had to go to an outside entrance. I put the key in the door to my room and walked in.

What did I find? I walked in on two people fooling around. I couldn't believe it. Never in my life had I been given an occupied room. It was scary. What if I had walked in on someone with a gun or on a couple of hoodlums doing a drug deal? I could have been shot.

I went back to the front desk. I was screaming, yelling, and swearing, using every combination of all the swear words I had ever heard. I threw the key at them and drove back to the "Hal" Suites. By now it was after midnight.

I said, "I am insulted. I can't believe what you have done. First of all, you insulted me by sending me to such a dump. I don't stay in places like that. Either you put me up in a five-star hotel this instant, or I sleep on that couch right across from the front desk, and by the way I sleep stark naked. If you want to get the police, get them, because I'm in the right. I have a confirmation."

At this point they must have thought they had a lunatic on their hands.

They kept telling me, "Calm down, calm down."

When they started calling hotels, the only place that had a room available was this fine hotel a few miles away, and the only thing *they* had available was the presidential suite.

The guy at the "Hal" Suites said, "It is very expensive."

I told him, "I don't care if it costs $10,000 per night. I'm not paying for it. *You* are."

It was 1:00 A.M. when I finally got to this hotel. My room was nice. I unpacked, and at 1:30 A.M., I finally got to talk to my girlfriend and find out how she was doing. Obviously, she was depressed, but at least I was able to talk to her instead of to a machine.

About 2:00 A.M. I finally got to bed, thinking "I have to get up in five hours."

I was just starting to doze off when I heard, "Bang! Bang! Bang!" on my door.

I thought, "What's this?"

I went to the door and looked out the peephole. I felt as if I had just dropped into a *Seinfeld* episode. What I saw was a naked man. I started laughing because not only was he naked, but with the convex lens, he was all distorted. *Every*thing was distorted. He was a big guy, and *every*thing was big. Now I was starting to laugh. I couldn't believe these things were happening to me. I felt that I was in Bizarro World!

I called the front desk and said, "Get Security up here. There's a naked guy at my door."

The voice said, "Yeah, right, sure."

I said, "Get up here now. There's a naked guy at my door."

A security guard came to my room and took the guy away. By this point I didn't want to go to sleep. I couldn't wait to find out what was going to happen next.

So far, in the past three hours I had been bumped from a hotel in which I was the speaker, I had walked in on people fooling around, and I had a naked guy pounding at my door.

I finally got to sleep.

The next morning I drove to the "Hal" Suites and went to the front desk.

I said, "I want to check in."

They said, "I'm sorry sir, it is 8:00 in the morning, and there are no rooms available."

I said, "Look, I know you have rooms available. People leave in the morning. If I have to jump over the desk and register myself, I will do it. Give me a room—*now*."

They give me a room. It overlooked a port authority and some gas tanks.

I thought, "No, no."

I went back to the front desk. They moved me again.

I finally told the people at the front desk, "You might want to come to the convention at noon today and attend my seminar. It is all about customer service, and I've decided to throw away my notes and talk about you and this hotel and what has happened to me, because I can't believe this experience."

They just looked at me.

I said, "Please do come, but don't wear your name tags because it will give away who you are."

Well, the rest of the time I was at that hotel, they couldn't do enough for me. That evening I got a phone call. "Mr. Becker, do you want tickets to the symphony? Do you want to rent some movies? What can we do for you?"

On my last day at the hotel, when I was getting ready to leave, the general manager called me to see how things were going. Where was he at the beginning of my experience? His phone call made me even angrier! Why didn't he call me sooner instead of later?

☑ What Should Be Done?

This answer is very easy. As soon as the hotel realized they were overbooked, they should have taken the initiative and solved the problem by reserving rooms for those guests at comparable hotels.

When I came in, they should have said, "Mr. Becker, yes, we have a small problem. We are in an oversold situation, but we have booked you a room at another nice hotel. We are going to provide you with shuttle service. Your car can stay here. Also, we are going to offer you dinner or breakfast. And when you come back, Mr. Becker, to compensate for the inconvenience, we are going to give you up to two nights free because we are so sorry this happened."

If they would have said that to me—instead of forcing me to ask for action and instead of putting me in a dump—I would not have considered it to be such a bad situation. But they did not use common sense.

With a little thought on the part of management, maybe even a quick meeting between the front desk and other hotel staff, this overbooking incident could have been prevented. The staff could have gone on the offensive instead of the defensive. They could have attacked the problem head-on instead of allowing it to get worse. The staff could have made the best of a bad situation, or may even have improved on it. But then this story never would have happened.

The funny part, in retrospect, is that because they did not do the right thing in the first place, the hotel management probably spent three or four times the amount for my room than they should have—they had to pay for my presidential suite at another hotel.

Oh yeah, the other, fine hotel faxed me letters of apology for the naked-man incident.

6 Retail Headaches

STUFF NOT FOR THE KITCHEN

For a moment let's look at the section of the store that's called the customer service counter. Why do we call it that? Do the people there perform customer service or customer inconvenience?

Usually fewer people are assigned to work at the customer service counter, and the lines are longer. If you don't believe me, just try to return a Christmas gift the week after. You might want to take a sleeping bag and be prepared to camp out in line, especially if it's a superstore!

People make constant fun of the U.S. Post Office. But recently we weathered a strike by UPS, and American businesses found themselves in quite a predicament when it came to shipping packages. As we all know, the U.S. Post Office picked up the overflow, and quite a huge overflow at that. But they were ready. They called it "Christmas mode." In post offices throughout the United States, the lines were kept short, and the packages got delivered in approximately the same amount of time.

So why can't retailers do a "Christmas mode"? It doesn't take a genius or a psychic to know that in the days immediately after Christmas, every store across the nation will be snowed under by long lines of people wanting to exchange and return merchandise.

Prepare for customer service and provide it. Don't just talk about it. Don't just slap a sign over a counter.

* * * *

I went to this home furnishings retail store because I needed to buy two wedding gifts, and I only had two minutes to do it. (Like most guys, I hate to shop, so I impose deadlines.) I ran in, selected two picture frames, and went to the counter for purchases to be shipped via UPS.

The counter had a fairly long line, with four or five people ahead of me. When I finally got waited on, the woman didn't have the foggiest idea of how to ship my purchase.

The manager came over and said, "Okay, I'm going to show you how to do this." And he actually began to explain the procedure to her. Ten minutes later I was still standing there, and now several people were waiting behind me.

In my nicest tone, I said to the manager, "Excuse me, is it possible that you could train her later? I'm in a hurry, and I don't know that this is the time to train her."

He said, "It's going to take just as long if I do it with her or without her. So you'll have to be patient. This is how we do our training."

He actually said that! His attitude was so snippy that I was just about ready to put the packages down, even after waiting all that time in line, walk out, and start all over somewhere else.

But there really wasn't anywhere else I could go, and I needed these gifts right away.

☑ What Should Be Done?

First, the manager should have said, "Absolutely, sir, you're 100% correct." He should have taken the order and rung it up quickly, because people were waiting behind me. He should train the employee when there aren't customers waiting.

Of course I believe in training. But this guy was training at the wrong time. Do the managers of professional sports teams train their athletes during a game in the middle of the season?

Second, this manager has never heard that the customer is always right, even when the customer is *not* right. The customer is in charge. *Never* talk back to a customer, especially in front of other customers.

This company needs to train its managers or replace them with managers who can do the job, because home furnishings is a very competitive market.

GENTLEMAN'S AGONY

This story is about a chain of men's clothing stores that has since gone out of business. I bought two shirts, and when I checked out, the cashier wouldn't smile. She didn't even look up at me. I knew it wouldn't do any good to tell her anything, so I went to the manager.

When I described what had happened and said she needed to learn about customer service, he just mumbled some excuse. He had a don't-care attitude.

☑ What Should Be Done?

If the manager doesn't care, how will the employees care? Again, as I've said, attitude is a very simple trickle-down effect.

When you hire a manager, hire an enthusiastic person who enjoys the job, and train that manager well. Put that manager on the floor to observe, teach, correct, and work with employees. Ensure that a positive attitude trickles down to your salespeople and other employees.

I find it amazing that with so much business out there and with *everybody* facing such stiff competition, that we still find so much of this "I don't care" attitude. I've said it before, a great company has great people. A company is only as good as its worst employee!

As I write this book, our economy is the best it has been in decades and unemployment is very low. So now the excuse is, "With unemployment so low, it's hard to find good people." The truth is that it has always been hard to find good people, but they *are* out there. Our job is to find them, train them, and then give them a reason to enjoy their job.

Treat the employee right, and they will treat your customers right. People want to feel good about themselves and have fun at work!

CANNOT HELP YOU
SPORTING GOODS STORE

■wanted simple knee pads for volleyball so I went to a sporting goods store that is part of a chain. Two employees were standing near the front door doing absolutely nothing. Correction: They were talking to each other.

I said, "Excuse me, where are the knee pads?"

They pointed to the far corner of the store and said, "Back there." Neither one made a move to lead me there and help. They needed a lesson from the Wal-Mart Stores—you know, the store with the greeters who walk you to the department.

I couldn't find the knee pads anywhere, so I went back to the front of the store. The two guys were still standing there, apparently nailed to the spot. I said, "Can you take me and show me?"

This request caused a great debate. I thought maybe they would flip a coin to see who lost. The two of them spent some time deciding which one was going with me.

Finally one of the guys said, "Okay, I'll do it."

I followed him. He showed me where the knee pads were, and then he promptly vanished.

I took a pair to the checkout line. Eight people were in line, but only one register was open. One clerk was at the register, and another employee was putting purchases into bags or just standing around waiting to bag items. A couple of other employees were walking by, but nobody was opening a second register.

When I finally got to the register, I gave the cashier a look of, "Gee, it's about time." The effort was wasted. She didn't look up at me. She didn't say anything—not a word. Not, "May I help you?" or "Thank you for shopping here" or "Have a nice day." Nothing. She just rang up the sale. Doesn't that make you want to run right back to this store?

☑ What Should Be Done?

The solution is obvious. One of the guys should have walked with me to the back of the store, and he should have asked me a few questions to help me pick the right product. To be really with it, he would have gone back up front with me, and when he saw so many people waiting in line, he would have gotten a second register open.

Months after I wrote this story, the company filed for bankruptcy and sold its assets to another large sporting-goods retailer. A lot of people will give you different reasons as to why this company closed its doors after decades of being in business. As far as I am concerned, almost all these sporting goods companies sell the same stuff and do it in good locations.

The problem wasn't location—the store was convenient. The problem was that it wasn't *fun* to shop there. In fact it was quite unpleasant.

What do you think it was like for the employees? Did they look forward to going to work every day? Many employees, the unlucky ones, say they *have* to go to work. Other employees enjoy going to work. It's up to senior management to establish the mood and tone of the working environment.

DUMMY'S AND HERMIT'S

had two experiences with these two sporting good stores. Both episodes happened when I was buying equipment to set up a gym in my house.

In the first instance, I was looking for a portable basketball system. I looked in the paper and saw that Dummy's had one for $209. I called them to check the price. Then I called Hermit's. They had a different system that they said they were selling for $219.

These stores are about three blocks from each other and fairly close to my home, so I went to both stores and looked at both systems.

What I found out when I got there was that each store was selling the product for less than the price they had quoted to me over the phone! Dummy's price was actually $189, not $209, and Hermit's price was $199, not $219.

I asked some questions in both stores. Nobody knew anything about the product or the price. At one store I asked for the manager, and even he knew nothing about the system. How can the managers train their people if they don't know the answers themselves?

☑ What Should Be Done?

Again, this episode is an example of what happens when a company hires people for $5 and $6 per hour and doesn't give them any training. The employees just walk around the store. They are selling high-tech products, like treadmills and workout equipment, but they have no training on the equipment. They know as much about their company's products as they know about nuclear physics!

Why do people who work at Wal-Mart and Target know so much about their competition in the discount retail business? Are these people exceptional? Do these companies have special connections or secret policies with respect to hiring?

No way. These companies simply hire people with the right attitudes, and then these companies train their people right and treat them right.

You and I know that any company can do the same. Maybe all middle managers and top management should work at a Wal-Mart or a Target for a few weeks as an entry-level employee to see how that company treats its people. Then those managers can go back to their own company and treat their own employees with respect.

DUMMY'S AND HERMIT'S (AGAIN!)

Every company has competition, and every company sells stuff for about the same price. So the choice boils down to this question: Where do you, the customer, want to shop? I myself want to shop at a store that treats me well, that is convenient, and that offers me a good selection at competitive prices.

* * * *

This incident happened at almost the same time as the previous story. I was looking for a sit-up board. Hermit's had one for $99. Dummy's had the exact same board for $79, but they were out of stock.

85

So I went back to Hermit's and said, "Would you be able to meet the price of your competitor?"

They said, "No, we won't do it." That was that.

I said, "You won't even meet the price of your competition?"

They said they couldn't.

I said, "Okay," and I walked out.

☑ What Should Be Done?

They should have matched the price. Period.

OFFICESTUFF

Ineeded three office chairs, so I went to OfficeStuff. I was ready, willing, and able to spend $1,000 on these chairs, so I was what's known in the profession as a real live prospect.

I walked around for 10 minutes trying to find someone to sell me chairs. Finally, I saw a guy who was taking care of another customer. I said, "Excuse me, can someone help me?"

He said, "I'll find someone soon." He actually said that! *Soon.* About five minutes later, he found a young woman, and he told me, "She'll be with you in a moment."

The young woman wasn't with a customer. She was sitting at a desk doing paperwork. The "moment" I was supposed to wait stretched into five minutes. Then the phone rang, and she answered it. She *still* hadn't even approached me.

I walked up to her and said, "Excuse me, please put that customer on hold."

She gave me a blank look, and that did it. I said, "I was going to spend $1,000 right now"—she kept giving me that blank look—"but obviously you don't have a clue on how to take care of customers." And I walked out. There are other places to buy office furniture.

☑️ What Should Be Done?

A problem like this one can be rectified simply by doing a time study to determine when you have your busiest times and how many people you need on the floor.

But however busy the staff is, they need to remember that the people who walk in to the store have priority because they are probably going to spend money *now,* faster than the people who call on the phone. If someone has driven or walked or crawled to your place of business, that person is a real prospect and very likely is ready to buy.

When the telephone rings, take a message for employees who are busy, or take the name and number and call the customer back, but the person in front of you needs to be taken care of *now.* So many companies and people need training in basic common sense!

Now you can see why I picked the cartoon for this chapter.

It is amazing to me that this kind of treatment is still prevalent. You can certainly understand why catalog sales, home shoppers clubs, and the like are becoming so popular. THEY TAKE THE HASSLE OUT OF SHOPPING!

The Internet will change the face of retail in the next 10 to 15 years. Retailers are in for quite a shock when they wake up to a world with a whole different way of doing business (more on this phenomenon in my chapter on the future of customer service).

People want things fast. They want things now, not later. And we have less patience than we did 10 or 20 years ago. We are also demanding more than ever—and we expect it!

"JERRY! OVER THERE, NEAR THE ESCALATOR. I THINK IT'S A SALES CLERK. QUICK! LIGHT ANOTHER TIE ON FIRE!"

©The 5th Wave by Rich Tennant, Rockport, MA. E-mail: the5wave@tiac.net.

HIGH-INCOME MALL

have been saying for years, "Technology is supposed to work
for us, not against us." It is supposed to make our lives
easier. And, for the most part, when technology is working, it
does make things easier.

But why do companies set policies that inconvenience
some of us or that take away our ability to make a choice?

And why do companies remove the human element? Sometimes I still enjoy talking to people and interacting with them. They can respond to me, they can tell me a story, or they can even talk back and upset me, but at least I have some kind of communication going. We can make eye contact and smile, and maybe this interaction will be my chance to learn something new for the day.

I want to be able to choose whether I deal with a human being or with a computerized system or the Internet. Maybe I've been cooped up too long, and I feel a need to talk to a real human being.

* * * *

First of all, I should say that I'm one of those people who never use an automated teller machine (ATM). I still use cash. Maybe I'm old-fashioned.

I wanted to buy a gift certificate that could be used at any of the stores in this mall, and I wanted to pay cash. The mall office refused to take my cash. I had to go upstairs to a little ATM. Not just any ATM—I had to use a specific one.

No matter what I offered, the woman in the office refused to take my cash. Nobody can get a gift certificate at this mall by paying cash. Here's another example of a system that has been created solely for the benefit of the company, and the customer can just put up with it—or get a gift certificate some-where else.

☑ What Should Be Done?

To this day, I'm still confused about this incident. I don't know why they insist on sending people to this one ATM. For whose benefit does this policy exist? For the consumer or for the mall office? Obviously, the important person is not the customer. It's somebody in the mall office. Priorities need to be straightened out here.

It would be very easy for the mall office to offer a gift certificate good at any of the merchants in the mall. By the way, this mall is not tiny. It must have about 200 merchants, including three department stores.

VERONICA'S DRAWERS

I went to Veronica's Drawers to get a gift. This retailer sells intimate apparel. The woman who helped me was wonderful, and it took me literally less than two minutes to find what I wanted. But then she just dropped me off at the counter, and I had to wait in line behind three other people. Only one clerk was working at the register.

Now I'm just a typical guy when I walk into a store like this. I will take the first thing I see just so I can get out of there as fast as possible and have more time to spend at a place that sells stuff with buttons or knobs.

Two employees were floating around the store. I stopped one of them and said, "Excuse me, are there any other cashiers here?"

She said, "No, the other cashier is at lunch, and this is the only cashier we have."

It amazed me that I had to wait in line for close to 10 minutes after it took me a minute and a half to find what I wanted. I almost walked out. The store didn't train other employees to use the cash register and instruct them to open another register when needed.

I find that approach to be incredibly shortsighted, making customers wait in line just to check out. If more customers had been there, we all would have had to wait even longer. Absolutely nobody else was able to ring up sales.

☑ What Should Be Done?

Here's an idea for a great experiment. Open a store called Vic's Store, cater to men, and just try making men wait in line to check out. I can tell you right now the store would close because it would have no sales.

I am thoroughly convinced that women are much more patient than men. Men will do anything to speed up the process. They will even say, "Okay, give me both shoes. I'll take the pair," just to get out of the store.

This waiting game is a poor system. Here are all these employees wandering around, doing nothing, while customers wait for service. A retail store should cross train its people so that several of them, not just one or two, can enter their code, open the register, and ring up a sale. This kind of cross training doesn't require a closet full of different kinds of designer tennis shoes.

Honda Corporation of America revolutionized the automotive industry when it opened the first Japanese plants in America. These transplants, as they are referred to in the automotive business, have cropped up all over the United States. Today we have Nissan, Toyota, Mazda, and even Mercedes-Benz and BMW.

These companies cross train their employees. Rather than keep someone on the production line for life, these companies rotate their people to a new position after a year. This rotation results in less monotony and allows employees to grow by learning about different aspects of manufacturing and about the plant they work in. In fact, employees can help each other become better by teaching coworkers about the job they just rotated from. The result is fewer defects and higher morale.

7 Feed Me! Love Me!

THE PERFECT RESTAURANT
FOR CAMPING

I love to go camping. One of my favorite places is Pymatuning Lake, on the border between Ohio and Pennsylvania. When I go camping, I take my tent, hatchet, precut firewood, starter log, inflatable mattress, sleeping bag, and portable television. Now *this* is *camping!*

After a night under the stars, I take down my tent, pack everything back in my car, and drive to breakfast. This Sunday morning, I was on my way home from camping, and I hadn't had breakfast. When it got to be 11:00 A.M., I realized I was hungry for some eggs. I stopped at two restaurants.

The first restaurant had a breakfast menu.

I asked, "Are you still serving breakfast?"

The waitress said, "No, we aren't."

I walked out.

At the second restaurant, I asked the waitress, "Are you serving breakfast?"

She said, "I don't think so, it's past 11:30, but let me ask the cook."

The cook was standing 15 feet away from me. The waitress asked, "Can you make eggs for this guy?"

He looked at me and said, "No."

✓ What Should Be Done?

I don't get it. Both these restaurants had a kitchen, and they had eggs, but they turned away a customer instead of serving a simple meal and making a few bucks.

Maybe we are all just making way too much money, or maybe the desire to make money is disappearing. Either way, I would rarely turn away good business, although I am a firm believer in getting rid of customers who drive me crazy or who are a pain in the neck.

But these restaurants didn't know me. I wasn't being a pain in the neck. My request was simple. I could have been a newcomer living in the town, someone who could be a repeat customer.

If you *can* do something for the customer, then do it! Making breakfast doesn't harm the ozone layer. It doesn't involve breaking one of the Ten Commandments. It's just a matter of breaking a couple of eggs. IT'S JUST BREAKFAST!

Give me a reason to want to come back. Give me a reason to talk you up, to tell other people about your company, and to give you the wonderful benefits of word-of-mouth advertising.

But if you happen to have more business than you can handle and don't want any more . . . then, hey, don't break any eggs for me.

GREASY'S

You know those trucks that deliver the eggs and bacon, the bread and butter, and everything else? Those trucks don't stop at just one chain. They make deliveries to the good, the bad, and the so-so.

Also, if you compare prices, you'll find that other restaurant chains can charge 20 to 35% more for the same items. Guess who has all the business: the great place, the one with the clean bathrooms, the friendly hostesses, and the reliable servers who have been with the same company for years if not decades.

You can charge more if you *do* more, and you can charge less if you do less.

* * * *

I don't know what I was doing at Greasy's. It wasn't 2:00 in the morning, so it wasn't as if this restaurant were the only place open. And it wasn't my birthday, so I didn't go there for a free meal.

But the other restaurant chain was busy, so we went to Greasy's. Nobody would seat us, so we found seats ourselves. We waited for six minutes while three waitresses stood around talking.

I was so ticked off that I did something I'd always fantasized about doing: I whistled. One waitress tore herself away from what obviously was the conversation of the century, and she came to our table.

I asked for menus, and she brought them to us. Then she threw the silverware on the table and walked away. She literally threw the silverware and the napkins on the table and walked away. So we walked out.

I couldn't believe it.

☑ What Should Be Done?

What do you think? It's Greasy's. Go to the other restaurant chain!

DON'T PLAY GAMES WITH ME TAVERN

I went to this restaurant for dinner with five friends, including Don Riemer, who is one of my best friends because he listens to me complain all the time! I was in the mood for a hamburger. The waitress said, "We don't serve hamburgers."

I said, "Please check with the chef, because I know that your other location has hamburgers on the menu."

She came out and said, "He doesn't really want to make a hamburger. He's pretty stubborn."

Don knew the owner and called him over.

The owner said, "No, we won't serve you a hamburger, because if we did, then 15 more people would want hamburgers."

To which I said, "Well, gee, then why don't you put hamburgers on the menu?" I got rather adamant about it.

The owner said, "You can order a hamburger at the bar, we'll turn our heads, and you can bring it over to your table."

I won't repeat what I was thinking. No way was I going to walk to the bar and carry back a hamburger. I did not order dinner, but I drank their water and I ate their rolls.

This restaurant, in a small New-Englandish type of town, may have good food and a devoted clientele, but while its owner has this attitude, it will never grow.

The only thing this owner cares about is policy. I am always amazed at how long places like this restaurant actually stay in business. I don't know why customers keep going back. Is it the location or the snob appeal?

If the restaurant had had a vegetarian menu or if they didn't serve hamburgers at all, I would have been more understanding. But they served hamburgers at the bar. What is so terrible about then serving a hamburger to a customer in the restaurant?

☑ What Should Be Done?

The solution doesn't require a rocket scientist—it's common sense. Don't turn a customer away.

My friends and I still talk about this incident. Why must some places be so difficult and others be so easy to get along with?

Again, I must emphasize that this restaurant serves food. It is not NASA. If this restaurant does not go by the book, we are not going to lose a space shuttle. If this restaurant bends a rule, we are not going to lose an astronaut.

Some people have to lighten up and realize their company is in business for just one reason: to serve people. It can be fun to please a customer and see a friendly smile on everybody's face.

THE ANGRY MEDITERRANEAN

I **went to meet some friends and have lunch at this upscale mall.** I went to The Angry Mediterranean in the food court and said, "I want a gyro sandwich and a glass of ice water."

The guy said, "Okay. A large cup?"

I said, "Sure, a large cup is fine." As I got my bill and walked away, I noticed that he had charged me a quarter for a cup of water. Now, the guy could have said, "I'm going to charge you a quarter for the water," but he didn't say anything, and the menu didn't say that they charged for water. I know the cup didn't cost a quarter.

There must be 20 other eating establishments in the food court. Will I go back to The Angry Mediterranean? Never again. For a quarter, they lost a customer.

By the way, four months later, I noticed they were gone from the food court.

☑ What Should Be Done?

The guy should have just said, "We would be happy to." He should have given me the drink at no charge. Period.

When you try to make the pennies add up, sometimes the result is that you lose the customers' dollars.

This scenario is a perfect example of an employee who either was not trained to use his head or was ordered to go by the rules and leave his brains at home. All he had to do was to go up to the manager and say, "Could we do this?"

In this case I know the manager would have said, "Absolutely, yes."

When I told the manager about what happened to me, he was furious with the employee. In fact you would probably recognize this employee because I think the manager took his head off. This situation could be turned around in about three minutes if handled properly by management. By the way, yelling is not proper handling, because yelling at people rarely motivates them to correct their actions. And *never* yell at *anyone*, especially in public!

Motivated employees *always* outperform unmotivated ones. Now this observation is hardly an original thought. It's obvious if you go into business establishments with any regularity. Despite the truth of this observation, most managers act as if the opposite is true. They yell at their people, talk down to them, and belittle them. Most managers abuse their power.

Everybody in a business—and I mean everybody—should read one of the classics in management books: *The One-Minute Manager* by Ken Blanchard.

Ken Blanchard's book takes just a couple hours to read, and it teaches four simple things:

1. Look for things that are right. Yes, that's correct. Look for the good, not always what's wrong.
2. Practice one-minute praisings. Do these in public if you like to make your employees feel good.

3. Practice one-minute reprimands. Always do these in private, and stick to the specific issue at hand.

4. Set one-minute goals. Let your people know what goals you have set for them, and find out what your people want and expect.

FANCY SCHMANTZY

Fancy Schmantzy is a fancy lunch restaurant, and I'm not a **Mr. Fancy.** I'm pretty simple. In fact, if the menu doesn't have pictures, I'm not comfortable. But I was meeting two rather important people over lunch, a magazine publisher and my publicist, and they had picked the place.

I looked over the menu, and nothing appealed to me, especially because I wasn't that hungry. I'd had breakfast and I didn't want a big lunch. So I asked the waiter for a small dinner salad.

He said, "No, the only salads we have"—and he pointed to the menu—"are the salads that are on the menu, and they are all big salads."

"Is it possible that I can have a small one?" I asked.

He said, "No, you can't."

I decided not to order anything. Each of the two people with me ordered a standard lunch that started with a small salad.

When their salads arrived, I started fuming. I kept staring at the waiter, but he just didn't get it.

When we were ready to leave the restaurant, I found the owner and said, "Let me tell you what happened." After I went through the whole scenario, I said, "I will never come back here again, and you had better talk to your waiter."

☑ What Should Be Done?

All the waiter had to do was to say, "Yes, we can do it, and it will cost this much," and I would have said, "Fine."

My request was so simple, because the two people I was with were served the very kind of salad I wanted.

Who is at fault in this situation? Is it the waiter, who just didn't think? Is the owner, who either has provided zero training for the employees or sets unreasonable policies?

This situation was so stupid that I later wondered if *Candid Camera* was there filming it. But since no one has contacted me or sent me any release forms to air this segment, they must have decided not to use the footage.

Again, all we are talking about here is a salad, not a satellite. It's just a salad! I wasn't going to eat the restaurant out of all its lettuce. I wasn't asking them to fly in the most trendy exotic lettuce on the Concorde. They didn't have to gut and renovate their kitchen to accommodate me. All I wanted was a plain and simple salad.

TOO MANY HUMANS

It was the weekend of a terrible blizzard. I ordered two dinners to go, no big deal. Their orders to go take usually take just 10 minutes, but this night they said it would be half an hour. With the blizzard, I wasn't surprised.

When I got there half an hour later, at least seven people were sitting in the waiting area. There was one waiter in the place, period. I saw my order sitting on the counter, with my name on the receipt, all ready to go.

I said to the waiter, "Excuse me, is this mine?"

He said, "One minute, one minute."

Instead he went and took orders at the tables. Almost 10 minutes went by. Then the people at one table asked for more water, and he went to get them water, which took another two or three minutes. Then he came out with more rice.

I said, "Excuse me."

He gave me the one-moment-please signal. Now, most people consider this the polite one-finger signal, but to me there's very little difference between fingers.

I finally turned to the people waiting with me and asked, "What's going on here?"

They said, "We don't know. It's unbelievable how bad this service is. We've been here for quite a while."

"Is it that bad?" I asked them.

They answered, "Yes."

I said, "Okay, watch this."

To the waiter I said "Excuse me" one more time.

The guy gave me the one-moment-please signal again. I turned to the people waiting to be seated, gave them an unprintable message for the waiter, and walked out.

I went home and ordered a pizza. They said it would be about 45 minutes. I guessed I'd rather have pizza.

During this entire episode, one thought kept running through my mind: "This scene is pure *Seinfeld*." If I hadn't been so hungry and frustrated, this whole episode would have been hilarious.

☑ What Should Be Done?

Management needed to give its people one short session on prioritizing. Those of us waiting could see that this one waiter had to do everything. We weren't being unreasonable. But it would have taken him one minute, literally one minute, to ring up my order and get me out of his life. But again, this place offered no training in Common Sense 101.

Sure, I understand that a business can be short of staff, especially when a blizzard or other situation results in staff not being able to make it in to work. But having just this one waiter was laughable, and it amazed the other people who were waiting along with me. In fact, you could call the episode a bonding experience. If we had exchanged phone numbers, we might be good friends today.

True, we were having a blizzard. But if you stop to think about it, we get snowed by some emergency or other just about every day of the year. With a quick meeting or a one-on-one session with staff, the manager could turn a negative situation, the weather, into a good experience for all of us—those who came in to work and those, like me, who were so unable or unwilling to cook that we went out into a blizzard to eat dinner!

8   This Is Service?

ROYALTY GAS CREDIT CARD

I've had a gas credit card under my name, The Becker Group Inc., since August 1985. I use this card for business expenses, and I'm the only person who uses it.

When I got my 1996 card in the mail and tried to use it in those little swipes that let you pay at the gas pump, I discovered that the magnetic strip on the card wouldn't work. The cashier told me to call customer service.

I called customer service three times. Each person I talked to argued with me that my card should and could work. I couldn't get anywhere with them. I asked for the manager, and each of them refused to connect me.

They said, "There's no manager on duty" or "I can't do that."

I had to get belligerent, and I finally got to the manager. Well, she said she would get back to me, but five days later, she still had not called me back. So I called again and got the voice mail from hell. I had to go through about 63 buttons on the voice mail before I could finally reach a manager, and that person wouldn't talk to me until I gave my account number. A different manager finally came on the line, and I told her the problem.

She said, "I will take care of it and get back to you."

I thought, "Let's wait and see." I said, "I don't care how you take care of it. I don't care what name is on the card. I just want my card to work in the machine."

Both managers did get back to me the next day, with an application for fleet manager privileges. I had to fill out the form for a fleet manager firm. What am I—an admiral? the owner of a trucking company? I said, "Screw it."

I went back to the gas station and filled out an application form for a card in my own name. I couldn't believe that after being a really good customer for 11 years I'd get such lousy service. What a company!

In about a week, I got a credit card in the mail. It was in my name, Hal Becker. About three weeks later, I got a letter and new cards for the Becker Group. The letter said that the company had a problem with their system and so they were reissuing the cards. I threw away my personal Hal Becker cards and went back to my original Becker Group cards.

☑ What Should Be Done?

All this confusion and difficulty could have been very simply avoided at the beginning, if only my original call had been transferred to a manager who said, "Let me check what's going on. I'll call you right back," and then did so.

The company probably already knew about the computer glitch. The manager could have said, "It will take three weeks (or four or whatever) to work out this software problem. We can send you an application for a personal card, or you can get an application from your local gas station, whichever you prefer. We really value your business, and to show you that, we are sending you a $10 coupon for gas."

Be honest, tell me the problem, and work with me. Then I would have said, "At least Royalty Gas is trying to fix this problem, and I understand."

But no, the company gave me the runaround and made me go through the trouble of finding a solution. I felt like they were just trying to irritate me.

Every time I use my card, I *still* think about how inept this company is. They care more about their advertising promotions than they do about their customers.

For me, this situation is the eternal dilemma: poor customer service vs. great location. I still go to this gas station on a regular basis. I don't know anything about gas, but I do know a good location, and this station is very convenient to use.

What can I do? Just hope and pray that another problem doesn't arise with this company so I have to go through the situation again.

I can also hope that the people in the Gas Station Location Department transfer to the Customer Service Department and try to improve that area.

AMERICAN SHIPPING SERVICE

Life has lots of stupid little annoyances. This episode is one of them. I go to American Shipping Service (ASS) every few weeks to ship books to customers and companies that order them.

The guy behind the counter was great. My problem started when I went to fill out the forms.

ASS has two kinds of forms. If you're sending one item, you use a small form with one box for "from" and one box for "send to." If you have more than one item, ASS has a larger form with one box for "from" but four "send to" boxes. This larger form is convenient if I'm sending packages to many different companies or if I'm sending many books to the same company.

Well, ASS had been out of these large forms for about two months now. When I came back this time, I thought for sure they would have the large forms, but hope, all they had were the small forms. So I stood there for about 15 minutes, filling out eight short forms instead of two large forms.

All my inconvenience was because ASS wouldn't reorder a simple form. Now, would that task have been easy to do? Yes. Would it make the customers much happier? Yes. Isn't it a simple matter to reorder the form, even if they have to reprint it? I'm sure it is.

It's just a form. But when I leave ASS, I won't be thinking about how nice they were, or how my packages got where they were going, but how my hand hurt from duplicating all that information on a lot of small forms.

☑ What Should Be Done?

It's just plain ridiculous—no, insulting—for a company the size of ASS to be out of a basic form for two solid months. This ASS location should have called headquarters and asked them to send some new forms overnight. After all, delivery is their business.

I frequent this company at least once a month, and I rarely have any problems. In fact, I can't even think of one other time I have had a problem with ASS.

So because I do so much business with this company, I mentioned this annoying situation to the clerk at the counter and expressed my frustration. Well, he in turn told me about *his* frustrations, about how the staff is so overworked that they don't even have the time to make the simple phone call that's needed to resolve my frustration. Something is not right at this company. Work should not be this frustrating or complicated.

Who was responsible for resolving my problem? To this day I don't know, and neither does the harassed employee behind the counter.

AMPLE PARKING
APARTMENT COMPLEX

My garage at home is full, so I wanted to park my sports car in the garage at Ample Parking Apartments, an upscale

apartment complex in my neighborhood. I called them, and it wasn't easy to get through to a warm body. But finally, my phone call was returned.

"The cost will be $50 a month," the caller told me.

I said, "I don't know. That's too expensive." So I called a friend who does work for the Ample Parking management company.

He said, "I'll take care of it." He called me back and said, "It will be $30 a month." Great!

A couple of weeks went by, during which I placed two more calls about parking my car there. Still I didn't get a call back. When I finally reached someone, this person quoted me a price of $45.

"Well," I thought, "I hope I can park there for $30. After all, my friend said it's all arranged."

The parking situation finally did work out, but this company seems totally disorganized. Every time I call them—or try to call them—I go round and round over something that should be very simple. It's obvious that this company has absolutely no communication and that they have zero training.

☑ What Should Be Done?

It's simple. The people in this company need to communicate with each other so they can get their act together. Such organization shouldn't take more than a meeting once a year or so.

Ample Parking is not just a garage. It's a large, fancy-looking apartment complex. I try to imagine what it would be like to live there, but just thinking about it gives me nightmares.

Sometimes I wonder how certain businesses are run. It seems that some people *need* power; they need to control everything, or at least try to.

Instead of having constant miscommunications, situations in which nobody is talking to anyone else, manage-

The 5th Wave
By Rich Tennant

©The 5th Wave by Rich Tennant, Rockport, MA. E-mail: the5wave@tiac.net.

ment should let people be responsible for their own actions. That concept means that if someone makes a mistake, it's not the end of the world—let that person learn from it. In too many companies, one person controls everything, so as a result he or she is asked a zillion questions all day long and constantly has to tell people yes or no, do this or do that. That's not management. It's just an ineffective means of control.

AMPLE PARKING
APARTMENT COMPLEX (AGAIN!)

Oh, those poor tenants! the way they must be treated.
One thing I need to tell you about this property is that
the location is one of the best in the city, if not *the* best. It's ac-
cessible to freeways and right next door to an excellent shopping mall.

The problem is that this apartment property has virtually
no other competition except for a few condominiums. If competition were tougher, this property would have a lot fewer
tenants. But just as we put up with average-to-poor customer
service, this company's tenants put up with average property
management. They accept it.

A great business is run by great people. It's that plain and
simple.

* * * *

I don't know why I do it, but sometimes I keep going back to
the same company. I'm embarrassed to admit to this flaw.
Once a year the geese fly north, the buzzards return to Hinck-
ley (that's in Ohio), and I call Ample Parking to inquire about
parking there.

I wanted to renew my contract to park my sports car in
this garage. The cost was $30 per month, $180 for six
months—a fair price for an indoor, heated space.

The staff had so much turnover that I didn't know who to
call. So again I called my friend who does work for the management company.

He said, "Call Dottie. But she is not very good on follow-up. In fact, I always have to chase after her."

I called and left a message for Dottie, who didn't return my call. Four days later I called again and was told, "Dottie is no longer working here."

I said, "How long has she been gone?"

They said, "About two weeks."

So somebody there took a message for a person who no longer worked at the company, and nobody else got back to me. This customer service is not very efficient.

Things got even worse. I talked to someone who said, "No problem, we will get you the space."

She sent me a signed contract, and I sent a check for $30 a month for six months, that is, $180, and the signed contract. Done. Easy—or so I thought.

Next I got a message that the owner wouldn't accept the contract. All of a sudden he wanted another $10 a month, a total of $60. I was ready to go to small-claims court if I had to. It was the principle, not the $60; I had signed and sent a legal binding contract and a check, which I was sure they had cashed.

I also informed them that they would be in this book.

The owner decided to accept the $180. With no apology, nothing, the company sent me a blank parking sticker in the mail. I followed up by sending them my first book (do you remember the title?) and a little note saying it was good that they did the right thing.

☑ What Should Be Done?

The company should have taken my $180 and said, "Great." End of story. They could have raised the rent the next year. Once a contract is signed, that's the end of it; it's a deal.

This company obviously needs better communication. For one thing, the person who answered the phone should not have taken a message for someone who no longer worked there.

For another thing, when the owner discovered that my contract had been renewed at the old rate, he should have simply processed it. He didn't even have to put himself in the customer's place. All he had to do was to realize that a deal is a deal.

The funny thing is that I can't imagine why he was bothering with an account as small as mine when he had thousands of residential units to think about.

ARRIVEDERCI LANDSCAPING

Arrivederci **Landscaping was doing work for my next-door neighbor.** On this day in August, as the crew was passing between our houses, one of their lawn mowers picked up a stone, and it came through my window, just like a BB. I had a witness: Linda, senior vice president of Hal Becker's world. (Now you know my secret. I have an office in my home.)

I called my landscaper first because I thought that's who might have done it.

They said, "No problem, we will pay for the window, but we were there Tuesday evening, not on Wednesday."

I said, "Thanks, but I can't let you pay for something that's not your fault."

So I called Arrivederci Landscaping. Now I was familiar with this company because it was my snowplow contractor. They completely denied breaking my window or even the possibility that they had broken it.

They told me, "There's no way we could have done that, because the only way to get our lawn mower through that spot is by removing the grass catcher, and we can't take the grass catcher off our lawn mower."

So I waited at home with a camera until they came back again. (As you can see, I have plenty of spare time!) Well, I saw one of their workers taking the grass catcher off the lawn mower, and I took pictures.

Arrivederci Landscaping actually kept arguing with me, still saying they hadn't broken the window. Finally, after a series of very long and very stupid conversations, and after I mailed them a set of my "Gotcha!" pictures, the company admitted they were wrong and said they would reimburse me for replacing my window.

After I got the window fixed, I sent them a copy of the bill for the repair. I didn't hear from them, so I called them three times. They wouldn't return my phone calls. I tried sending a letter. No answer.

So I decided to try something a little tougher. By now it was November, and Arrivederci sent me a snowplow contract. The snowplowing cost $150, and the window cost $200. So I sent their contract back with a note saying they could either pay me for the window, in which case I would send them a check in full for the snowplowing, or else they could do my snowplowing for free and send me a check for the balance, $50. I thought that solution was simple and easy. No mess, no fuss.

Arrivederci Landscaping finally decided to send me a check for the cost of the window. The amazing thing was that they also returned my contract, with "null and void" written all over it. They acted like *I* was in the wrong! This scenario is one more example of a company with absolutely no idea of what customer service is all about.

☑ What Should Be Done?

What I find fascinating about this story is that two companies in the same business can have such totally different attitudes in the same situation. One attitude said, "The customer absolutely comes first," and the other attitude said, "We don't value your business."

My landscaper, without the least hesitation, said, "We will pay for your window."

I had to argue with them. I had to say, "I don't want you to pay for it because it wasn't your fault. You told me you weren't even there on the day it happened."

Now, Arrivederci had been my snowplow contractor, and they had done a good job. I had never had a complaint, and I had never needed to call them for any reason. Their plow came early in the morning and did the job perfectly. But this very same company was arguing with me, forcing me to take pictures, and forming an offensive-defensive relationship. None of these things should have happened.

The company should have offered me options, instead of my having to suggest options to them. The options didn't even involve much money. Arrivederci could have plowed my drive at no charge for one season. It would have been such a simple thing, especially because they had at least five other contracts right in my neighborhood.

Instead, the company voided my snowplow contract; they obviously didn't want to do business with me again. Call it stubbornness, a lack of common sense, or just basic stupidity—they lost the money and lost a customer.

When I talked to my neighbors, I found that they didn't like this company either, but some of them *still* use this landscaper. Why? because it's easier to put up with lousy service and a bad attitude than it is to take the time and effort to switch to another company.

We all do this. We get mad for the moment, and later we make an excuse for the company or the employee's attitude. We don't change companies until we get to our breaking point, which is much later or never.

I hope this book will cause more of us think twice and change vendors or companies a lot faster if we're unhappy. We also need to let *senior* management know why we left or are thinking of leaving, so maybe they can correct their way of doing business—and ensure that *every*body wins. Believe me, the best companies *want to know* when they or their people screw up, because those companies want to remain the best.

9 You Can Bank on It

LENDING-A-TON BANK

I do quite a bit of banking at Lending-a-Ton Bank. Why? Because they have a branch just two blocks from my office.

I can't tell you the exact amount, but I must have $40,000 just sitting in a checking account, keeping warm. (Yeah, yeah, I know it's stupid.) This day all I wanted to do was make a deposit. There were four people in line ahead of me, and only one window was open.

The manager, the person I usually see sitting at her desk, was now standing next to the teller at the one open window, and all five of us customers were staring at the manager, giving her the evil eye in the hope that we could make her open another window. But she was not opening another window. She was asking the teller when the other teller would be coming back.

There are things it's just not polite to say in public. So instead of saying anything, all of us kept standing in line and kept giving the manager a long, hard stare.

What I really wanted to do was to say, "Excuse me, is it beneath you to take care of a customer or two?" After all, managers go through a training period that includes actually working as a teller.

But instead, it was more important to her to stand behind the teller, ask her a couple of questions, and shuffle papers rather than take care of customers. The scary part is that she is the manager.

Finally, I did say, "Excuse me, do you know how to work the equipment behind you?"

She said, "Yes, I do."

I said, "Well, then, get up and do it." At that point everyone in line with me started to applaud.

☑ What Should Be Done?

This episode is the first of three with Lending-a-Ton Bank. Up front let me say that the problem with the banking business does not exist just in my bank in my community. It exists everywhere.

The tellers are in fact the most important people in a bank or a savings and loan because they are the ones who interact the most with customers. The problem is that tellers aren't trained, at least not beyond the absolute minimum, and they certainly don't get enough training in the area of customer service.

I don't know about you, but I don't bank with a machine. I never have and I never will, despite all the bank's efforts. And I think there are a *lot* more people out there who feel the way I do.

At any rate, tellers are not trained in common sense. By common sense, I mean doing the smart and simple thing that's needed to keep customers happy.

Smart businesses realize that without customers there is no business. So the customer comes first and foremost. Paperwork comes later. Lunch comes later—or earlier. I find it unbelievable that during the busiest time of the day, lunchtime, a bank has the fewest tellers available. The tellers should stagger their lunch breaks.

Also, it amazes me how often bank personnel busy themselves with paperwork instead of opening another teller window when the line of customers starts to grow. Do bank people think their paperwork comes first?

Another thing: It wouldn't kill the manager if he or she had to work a window. Besides being good for customer service, this action would do wonders for employee morale. When employees see the boss working alongside the troops, the employees have a lot more respect for that manager.

Last of all, what still perplexes me is why *most* banks are so different from savings and loans. I know that different regulating bodies govern banks than govern savings and loans, but I can't for a moment believe that difference accounts for why the two institutions have such different attitudes.

When I go into a big bank, the message I get is, "Wait over there in line, Mr. Becker. Don't try to have any fun, and no smiling either. And please refrain from making eye contact with the tellers—they are very busy and way too professional to be nice."

When I walk into a savings and loan, the message I get is, "Hi, Hal! What's happening? How's the Rogaine working? Are you still trying to sell your Yugo?" The attitude seems a lot more personal, not because it's a smaller operation, but because the business is run with a more homey atmosphere.

Where would *you* rather visit?

LENDING-A-TON BANK (AGAIN!)

had just returned to the United States from doing a few seminars in the Philippines. While I was there, I had visited a state hospital, and I had been tremendously moved by the work its staff did under unbelievable conditions. In a children's ward, the beds consisted of a piece of wood and a blanket, and mothers were squeezing respirator bags by hand. I walked out of that place crying. I figured the least I could do was to make a donation to that hospital.

I wanted to make a donation in the form of a money order, not a personal check, because it might take months for a check to be posted. Now, I should say that Lending-a-Ton Bank has the pleasure of taking care of a lot of my money in a corporate checking account that doesn't bear interest.

There's one other thing I should explain at this point. All I do at this bank is go in once a month and make a deposit. No fancy transactions. No special requests. No long, drawn-out deals. I just go in once a month, give them money, and they give me this tiny receipt.

On this occasion, after I deposited almost $10,000, I asked the teller for a money order.

He said, "That will be a $3 charge."

I said, "Let me make this real easy for you. I just deposited almost $10,000 into an account that doesn't pay me any interest, and you want $3 for a money order. Either you don't charge me $3 for the money order or I will close my entire account immediately. Otherwise get me the manager now!"

The teller got the manager. Now this manager sees me every month.

I got my money order at no charge, but the manager said, "We're doing this for free just this one time only."

Of course. Unfortunately, this mentality is typical of a bank. Even more unfortunately, I just keep going back to the same bank. It's too much trouble to close the account, open a new one, get new checks, and all that.

As I said before, the most important people in a bank are the tellers, but they are the ones with by far the least training. The management must order them to follow simple procedures and, above all, to get the paperwork done.

☑ What Should Be Done?

The teller should have looked at the computer screen, which shows my account balance. The teller should have thought, "Boy, Mr. Becker has a lot of money in this account—and it's not bearing any interest. Is that stupid! We charge $3 for a money order, but he's such a good customer that he shouldn't have to pay $3. It would be an insult."

Are computers making us lazy and stupid, or do we not care any more? The purpose of computerization is to make us more productive and to put information literally at our fingertips any time we want it.

I know one thing for a fact. If there are computers in businesses where we as customers have accounts, then in most cases those computers can provide an array of information about us, the customers, or about our business transactions.

If you are the employee behind the counter or the desk in this scene, you need to step back mentally, think for a second, and remind yourself that the customer in front of you is a human being, like you. Now look at the computer screen and see what information will be *helpful* to this human being in the situation at hand.

Let's use automation to make us better and more prepared instead of being so quick to say, "I can't." I really think that some people use the computer as an excuse to say no, because they find it so much easier than *doing* something for the customer.

Then the teller should have said, "No problem, Mr. Becker. I just need to get a manager's approval to waive the $3 fee." (Better yet, the teller could just insert a code and automatically waive the fee, but that would be revolutionary, and we all know how conservative banks are.)

Second, the teller should be trained and empowered to give me good service. In this episode, the teller would look at the screen and think, "Boy, does this customer need help. He has more than $40,000 sitting in an account that's not bearing interest, and now he's depositing another $10,000. Wow!"

Then the teller should have said, "Mr. Becker, could we have one of our account executives call you to talk about some of the great places in which you can put your money to earn interest rather than keeping it in this type of account?"

But in this situation, a policy seemed to be more important than a customer. The teller couldn't even look at the screen and put two and two together. This scenario is another example of a company that offers no training, no common sense, and no empowerment to allow the tellers to take care of the customers.

LENDING-A-TON BANK (AND AGAIN!)

Once again, *who* exactly are the people for whom bank policies are created? When I open an account at a bank, do I lose all my rights as a customer?

It's funny how banks advertise. My bank has a slogan that says it's my "private banker," which I would think means that no matter what the size of my account, big or small, I should have my own private banker who calls me to ask how I am, to tell me how my money is doing, or to say, "Hey, stupid, get your money out of that lazy, unproductive checking account and put it where it can be working for you."

While my bank's ad sounds great, I'm sorry to say that I've never set eyes on this private banker of mine, nor have I had any dealings with any such person. This private banker has never called me or even sent me a letter. Nothing! (It's funny how many banks claim to be their customers' private banker!)

Imagine a bank that really puts the customer first. I see no waiting lines when I walk in. I see tellers that take the time to get to know me and review my account. That's what I want, not some stupid toaster or clock radio or picnic cooler. Keep the gifts. Just make me feel like a good customer.

I went into the bank to deposit more than $15,000. I thought, "While I'm here, I'll exchange some foreign money into U.S. currency." I had about $200 in Philippine money, which probably was about $10 in U.S. money, and a $20 Canadian bill. I deposited the check, and then I asked the teller to exchange the currency.

She gave me a blank stare and said, "Do you have a personal account here?"

I said, "No. I just have a corporate account."

She said, "I'm sorry, we can't exchange the currency."

I said, "Excuse me, I just gave you $15,000. Even if you can't exchange the Philippine currency, you can at least give me $14 U.S. dollars for this $20 Canadian bill." Then I said, "Get me the manager, please."

The manager came up and said, "Are you a sole proprietor?"

I said, "Yes, I am."

She said, "Well, okay."

Well, not so okay. They had me do a lot of paperwork. I had to fill out a form in triplicate with my name, phone number, and address. I had to sign it to get $14. In the meantime, I had given them $15,000, for which they had given me a tiny receipt the size of a business card! Who put this plan together? Is this good customer service? I'm not sure.

☑ What Should Be Done?

Excuse me, but my phone is ringing. I think it might be Lending-a-Ton Bank asking me—after reading this book—to be their vice president of customer relations. Or they might be asking me to transfer my account to another bank.

This episode should never have happened. The teller should have just looked my account balance on the teller screen, made a simple decision, and then looked at me and said, "Yes, Mr. Becker, no problem. We will be happy to do that for you."

127

Obviously, the person who makes decisions about forms and policies and procedures hasn't been clued in on the subject of customer service. If everybody in management had to get in the trenches every once in a while to see what happens there, I wonder if episodes like this would ever happen again. I also dream about what a Ritz-Carlton bank would be like.

I might get into the *Guinness Book of Records* as the first person to be asked by a bank, "Sir, can you please take your money elsewhere?"

10 Death and Taxes

BUCKEYE TELEPHONE COMPANY

Unbelievable! Buckeye Telephone Company is my phone company for local service, but they were telling me that I have to get my voice mail hooked up by another company who is my long-distance carrier. Once upon a time, Buckeye Telephone Company was my long-distance carrier, but thanks to our judicial system, all that is history, and everything that was simple and easy is now confusing and complicated.

All I wanted was voice mail. Very easy—or so I thought. I called Buckeye Telephone Company and told them what I wanted. I have two lines that hunt to each other, as the jargon goes. If both lines are busy or if there's no answer, I wanted the call to go into voice mail. The cost was about 50¢ per line per month, and it would take the phone company about a second to flip a switch and make it happen.

The first guy I talked to was real nice. He said, "No problem. That's very easy to do. You'll have it in a couple of hours."

I waited two days. Then I called Buckeye Telephone Company. I sat on hold forever, so I hung up again and dialed again. The same thing happened. The third time I dialed, I finally got a human being. But he had no idea of how to do what I wanted—and he actually disconnected me.

I thought, "Somebody who works for a telephone company should not be disconnecting me."

The fourth time I called, a woman said, "I'm sorry, we can't do this service. You have to call the other company."

Obviously, she was clueless. She *could* do it. What kind of training do these people have, that I had to argue with them to get something very simple done?

I said, "Do you have a supervisor?"

"No, we don't," she replied.

"You're telling me you have no supervisors there?" I asked.

She said, "That's correct."

I imagined blind people walking around without seeing-eye dogs. At this point, Mr. Nice went out to lunch and Mr. Mean came on the scene.

I said to her, "Look, you tell me there's nobody there but you. So let me tell you what you have to do." And I launched into what I call telephone tech-talk. "Put call-forward-no-answer on both lines and call-forward-busy on the second line." I was explaining to her how to do her job.

Well, an hour and a half after this conversation, I had my voice mail. So I guess the moral here is that you need to know your stuff, read all the technical manuals before you call, and then nicely and to the point tell them what to do, or you'll never get your service done in a normal amount of time.

☑ What Should Be Done?

This story is a classic example of poor training. A lot of companies have this idea that their experienced people are costing too much in salary and benefits and that the company can make more money if it replaces these expensive employees with inexperienced people. The new people don't get any training, and they don't learn enough about the company's new products, which are what the customers want.

Some great software products could help Buckeye Bell's employees serve their customers. For example, General Electric has an impressive system that brings pictures and diagrams up on the computer screen, making it easy for an employee to explain a process or product to a customer.

With computer technology, a company could have a software system that deals with frequently encountered problems or situations and that gives the employee a script with various options.

It was obvious that the people I talked to were just winging it; they did not have a clue. It's shameful that a regular customer—and I'm a regular everyday guy, not someone who wears a pocket protector with 25 color-coded pens—has to be more experienced than the Buckeye Telephone Company employee who's supposed to be an expert on the subject.

What really frustrates me is this: I am finding that the more I know about particular subjects, products, or services, the more I find myself educating the person who is supposed to be *taking care of me*. I'm doing the company's work—and I'm paying!

What's next? Will I be telling my doctor which way to do an operation, or when to use a laser instead of a scalpel?

When I visit or call on a business, I want *them* to tell *me* what I need or what I should do. I don't want to have to decide—or to wonder whether they are making stuff up.

The more training people receive, the better they are. As a result, they will enjoy their jobs more, and even better, they may care about their jobs more and want to satisfy the customer more—not just go through the motions or put in another day on the job!

AMERICAN PHONE & EQUIPMENT (AP&E)

This story too is beyond belief. I went to the AP&E phone store to order caller ID. All my friends were having fun sitting around Saturday night screening their calls, so I thought, "I'll get caller ID too."

No big deal. The clerk at the phone store hooked me up directly to Buckeye Telephone Company. I talked to Buckeye's

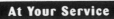
customer service and ordered caller ID. The employee told me about the promotion Buckeye was running, which was one free month and no hookup fee.

I said "Great. Let's do it."

I needed a caller ID box, and I had seen an ad by a company that was selling caller ID boxes for $10 cheaper and that was right across the street from the AP&E store. When I was at the AP&E store, I said, "Can you match your competitor's price, seeing as I am here placing an order for caller ID to work on my phone."

They said they couldn't.

About 10:00 the next morning, I decided to call Buckeye Telephone Company back and double-check on my order, because I know that orders can get screwed up.

Buckeye had absolutely no record of my order. Nothing. They didn't have any idea. So I had to place my order all over again.

I told them about the special.

They said, "Oh yes, we have that special."

This is Buckeye Telephone Company, part of the corporate backbone of our nation. It scares me to think that we might have to go back to using two tin cans and a long string.

☑ What Should Be Done?

By the way, AP&E stores are gone. They don't exist.

The clerk at the AP&E store should have been able to place my order and to send it directly to Buckeye Telephone Company so it could be hooked up, billed, and so on. And the store should have been able to match the competitor's price. So not only did I have to go round and round, but I also couldn't get the best price.

The store should have said, "Yes, we can match the price, no problem," and then they should have put a note on the or-

The 5th Wave   By Rich Tennant

In a chance meeting prior to their singing careers, Carreras, Domingo and Pavarotti all worked at the same customer service phone center.

"WHOA, WHOA, FELLOWS. TONE IT DOWN! WHAT ARE YOU TRYIN' TO DO, IMPRESS SOMEONE?"

©The 5th Wave by Rich Tennant, Rockport, MA. E-mail: the5wave@tiac.net.

der that this price was a special exception and that they were matching a lower price. But the store just really didn't care about making a sale. The episode was another example of poor training and poor communication.

People think that bigger is better. Sometimes it is. Wal-Mart and Home Depot have proved that, as have a number of other superstores. But bigger is not *always* better.

Yes, the bigger companies have more money. They can do better research, they can open with more inventory, and they can do more advertising and marketing.

If that's so, why do some big companies open and close almost as fast as Peppi's Pizza? If we look at the number of large business-to-business corporations that have tried retailing, we see that a great number have failed. The list includes IBM, Xerox, and Digital Equipment.

Instead of trying to corner *all* the markets, why don't big businesses just try to be the best at what they already do best? Improve on the core business. A company's greatest asset is its people. Concentrate on them, focus on the basics, and you'll find yourself excelling in your own ballpark and being the best in your field.

Many companies—including Sears, Xerox, Ford, and Kmart—tried to enter fields that weren't their niche but failed, losing money and people. Know your strengths and use your focus to build on them.

LAKE ERIE POWER

I decided to call Lake Erie Power when I got my electric bill in the mail. It was a high bill, $198.09, and normally I just don't get high bills.

I looked at the bill carefully. It was for 59 days, and there was no reading for August or September. The back of the bill said that customer service hours were 7:00 A.M. to 7:00 P.M.

It was about 6:20 P.M., and I thought, "This will be a great time to call, while everyone's eating dinner."

I waited on the phone for 18.5 minutes—I know that because I have a timer on my phone. It took 18.5 minutes until I got a live voice, and all the while they were playing all those little customer-service jingles about how they want to take care of you. It was like being in an elevator with the Muzak from hell.

I was just laughing while I was on hold and being ignored. I don't think anyone should have to wait 18.5 minutes just to ask a couple of questions. I just wanted to find out if they received my check after they mailed me this bill.

I finally got a human being, who told me that either the meter reader never came out that one month or else the reader had had a problem reading my meter, and it wasn't read until the next month.

I had an easy and simple question that took about 30 seconds to answer, but first I had to wait 18.5 minutes on hold.

☑ What Should Be Done?

This episode is a combination of good and bad. Once I reached a live human being, that person was obviously well-trained and able to handle my problem immediately. But to wait on the phone for more than 18 minutes is *not* good.

Why companies call this department Customer Service is a mystery to me. They should rename it *Customer Aggravation*.

With so many businesses saying, "We believe in customer service," we customers should have very few hassles and our lives should be simple. But we don't, and they aren't.

This anecdote is a great example of why we all make so much fun of utility companies and the frustrations we have with them.

Picture this scenario: The CEO of this utility company— let's call him David—lives in a house, just like you and me, and he has a question about his bill. His friends are visiting, and they say, "Dave, tomorrow call your own company. Pretend you're one of us. Just call the number on the back of your bill. If *you* had to wait 18 minutes to get through, wouldn't you order a special meeting to be called the first thing the next morning to discuss this problem and solve it?" So, CEOs and managers, CALL YOUR BUSINESS TOMORROW, PRETEND TO BE A CUS-

TOMER WITH A QUESTION OR A COMPLAINT, AND SEE WHAT IT'S LIKE TO BE ONE OF THE LITTLE PEOPLE!

Wait a Minute

Yesterday, I called Internet onhold, the Internet service provider. I had a question. I got their voice mail. The non-human voice said, "Your call will be taken in approximately 9 minutes or more."

I figured there must be a way to get help sooner, so I started punching buttons. I tried every menu I could find, but I kept getting that same message, except that each time the wait got longer. I went through *seven* different menus, and each time I got that message, and finally the nonhuman voice said, "Your call will be taken in approximately *15 minutes* or more."

What does that tell me? If callers have to wait this long, the company should be conducting nonstop hiring and training. But obviously once Internet onhold gets the customer's money, the customer is no longer important.

THE PLACE WHERE YOU MAIL STUFF AT

First off, let me say that I am a big fan of the The Place Where **You Mail Stuff At.** People make fun of it and badmouth it, but the The Place Where You Mail Stuff At delivers approximately 183 billion pieces of mail per year—that's about 603 million pieces per day—to more than 120 million addresses across the United States.

So when you hear somebody say, "The check is in the mail" or "I mailed it yesterday," consider the source. How many times in the past five years did you *not* receive your bill from the phone company, gas company, or electric company?

The bottom line is that the The Place Where You Mail Stuff At does a pretty good job delivering the mail. Now, as for dealing with a problem, that's a whole other ball game!

When I moved into my new house, I still had not sold my old house. I had to fill out a change-of-address form. But when I went to my old house to make sure everything was okay, my mail was still being delivered there. I filled out a second change-of-address form, but—you guessed it—my mail was *still* being delivered to my old address.

I guess I was lucky I didn't sell my old house right away because eight months after I had moved, my mail was still being delivered to the old address. I left a note for the mail carrier at the old address, saying I had moved. The carrier just pushed the note aside and kept delivering the mail there.

I called the supervisor and told him the problem.

He said, "I will take care of it."

He didn't, so I called again. No results.

When I called for the third time, I jokingly said, "Please do me a favor. Please hit the mail carrier over the head for me."

The supervisor said, "I'm sorry, we can't do that."

Whew! I think this supervisor needs a sense of humor. Or else he needs to loosen his tie so the blood can get to his brain.

☑ What Should Be Done?

The company should have said, "No problem, we'll take care of it." Then they should have taken care of it and followed up to let me know everything was fixed. Just put it in the system and do it!

11 The Finer Things of Life

VERY EXPENSIVE CLOSETS

I was really hyped up and looking forward to the first of October. I couldn't wait for the salesperson from Very Expensive Closets to come to my house. It wasn't just that I needed to get my closets organized, as important as that was. This company sent a letter to confirm the appointment, and everything they did and said sounded great. So I was really looking forward to dealing with this company.

Steve, the salesperson, came to my house, spent an hour with me, and asked a ton of questions. He was a really upbeat guy and did a great job. I was totally impressed. There was just one detail I had a question about. The company's payment policy was one half before installation and the balance after installation.

I asked, "Can I just pay the whole thing when the guys walk in the door to do the installation? A COD type of transaction?"

Steve said, "Yeah, you got it, no problem."

The next day, I got a message on my voice mail from someone named Donna saying, "We cannot schedule installation because we have not received our down payment yet." She was very matter-of-fact.

I called Donna back and said, "I talked to Steve. He suggested that I could pay in full at the time of installation."

She said, still very matter-of-fact, "I'm sorry, we can't do that. This is our policy."

I said, "Well, Steve told me I could."

She said again, "I'm sorry but this is our policy." Then she said, "If you want to, you can send a check in full ahead of time."

I said, "No, I don't pay for installation on a contracting job before it's done." I was very angry. As soon as I hung up, I called the company back and left a real nice and very detailed message on their general voice mail saying how professional

Steve was, but that I was thinking of canceling the installation because this nonsense about payment was taking the fun out of this experience, and because a deal is a deal and they should honor it.

Steve called me back and left a message saying, "I got your message. No problem, but they still would like to have a credit card number."

I called back and told Steve I was uncomfortable with that arrangement, that a deal is a deal. We finally got this thing resolved. Then I had to wait two weeks until they could install the closet. The installation went smoothly. It was great. They more than doubled my closet space, and I even got a new tie rack. It's a cool system!

☑ What Should Be Done?

For the point of this story to kick in, we must revisit the introduction of this book and look at that statement that "the customer is in charge." I was so excited for this project to happen, but this one employee, Donna, took all the fun out of it. Her attitude made me, the customer, *expect* things to go wrong instead of right and even to start looking for problems.

The frustrating part is that this company is supposed to be top-shelf (pun intended), the best in their business. This company has quality products and quality installers, but something less than quality people in the office.

Donna should have said, "Yes, Mr. Becker, if that's what Steve said, fine, no problem. You can pay upon installation." Or, "Could we have a credit card number to hold until your check clears?" Those answers would have been easy. But no, she had to give me a difficult time.

I would love to recommend this company to my friends but I can't. I am very happy with my closets. The company definitely doubled my closet space. They did everything they were supposed to do from an installation point of view, but in other respects this company had poor communication and follow-up.

This company is obviously a small business in which everything starts at the top with the local owner or franchisee, so the lines of communication should not get this confusing.

This company needs to train its people in how to deal effectively with customers, how to listen to them, and how to find a way of saying yes instead of just saying no.

My salesperson was very upbeat and enthusiastic, and he was very good about showing up on time for the appointment, but he did not follow through on a couple of things that he promised to do.

For example, he promised to bring a rack for me to hang my clothes on while the closets were being installed. He didn't. And he didn't stop by during the installation, which he had said he would do. He may think he is a good salesperson, but when you look at the total picture, he really isn't.

This company could be easily turned around because it has a superior product, good advertisements, good quality. The installation people were phenomenal.

Improvement is just a matter of getting the office staff together on an ongoing basis, once or twice a month, so four or five people in sales and administration can meet with the owner in the same room and have a much-needed discussion about how to do things better.

Better: That's the key word.

COLD WATER HOT TUBS

This occurrence is about a cover for my hot tub. Eight weeks after I had ordered a cover for my hot tub, the cover still hadn't arrived. I called Cold Water Hot Tubs.

The woman who answered the phone said, "Let me check in the back." She came back to the phone and said, "Yes, it's here. We will call you back with a delivery date."

At this point I thought, "How long has the cover been sitting there? And would they ever have delivered it if I hadn't called them?"

Five days later, I still hadn't heard from Cold Water Hot Tubs, so I called back. I talked to the same woman.

She said, "Well, we will have someone call you and let you know when we can deliver your cover."

Another two days went by, and I still didn't have a delivery date. The cover was sitting there, at Cold Water Hot Tubs. Correction: *my* cover—I had already paid $400 for it.

Why would anybody want to do business with a company like this? Hassling this company for a delivery date is no way to spend precious leisure time.

The owner of Cold Water Hot Tubs is a nice, likable guy. He hires a lot of seasonal employees and part-time help and pays them mostly minimum wage. This fact, however, is no excuse for the lack of training or communication.

☑ What Should Be Done?

I'm sure that I'm not the only customer who needed to have an order tracked. Cold Water Hot Tubs needs a simple system for tracking orders. I had to hound the company and fight with them to get my delivery. Otherwise I might never have received my hot-tub cover.

What the company should have said and done is, "We are so sorry for the inconvenience. Here's a $50 gift certificate to our store." They didn't have to make such an offer, but an apology and a gift certificate would have made me want to go back to them, and the experience would not have left a bad taste in my mouth.

Cold Water Hot Tubs would have been way ahead. The lowest-priced item in the store is about $300, so a $50 gift certificate would have brought them more money.

This situation requires simple common sense. You can have all the mission statements in the world. You can talk until you're blue in the face about empowerment. These actions don't mean anything unless you have ongoing training sessions and follow them up with actions.

I wasn't an unhappy customer. I was a frustrated customer. I knew this company was a good company and that it wasn't a question of *if* they would do the right thing for me, but *when* they would do it.

With a simple system, a little training, a bit of niceness, and some common sense, Cold Water Hot Tubs would have made a frustrated customer really happy, and they would have had another sale.

Some company owners and managers make the mistake of focusing on the small picture instead of the big one.

Cold Water Hot Tubs spends quite a chunk of money on advertising. Instead, they should let the customers sell the company to their friends. After all, this company sells not just hot tubs and chemicals, but also pools, patio furniture, pool tables, fireplaces, and home gyms. With such an extensive product line, the person who walks in to buy any one of these products could wind up being a customer for life!

Imagine the outcome if, instead of just advertising products and prices, this company were to concentrate on exactly what it would take for me to *want* to come back and for me to always think of this company when I think of its products. Cold Water Hot Tubs would enjoy higher margins, more customers, lower advertising bills, and lower employee turnover. These benefits would happen because the company would enjoy selling to the same people over and over and selling to *their* friends and family.

Companies should look at the long-term picture, not just the month-to-month one.

LAKE ERIE BOTTLED WATER

I wanted to give one of my closest friends a six-month supply of bottled mineral water and one year of cooler rental as a housewarming gift. Lake Erie Bottled Water supplies water to businesses and homes, and I'd had an account with Lake Erie for about 14 years. I called their customer service.

I said, "I would like to give my friend six months of water and a year of cooler rental, and I want to pay for it in advance."

The woman in customer service said, "I'm sorry sir, we really can't do that. If you want to pay for the six months, I need all the information from your friend so we can do a credit check on her."

I couldn't understand why they had to check my friend's credit if I was the one paying. Besides, this gift was a surprise.

I said, "No, I want to make this easy."

"I'm sorry sir, we can't do that," she replied.

So I said, "Fine, I'll call the owner," and she said, "Okay."

When I called the owner, he did the right thing. He called me back within the hour and said, "We just had a Hal Becker meeting," meaning they had just had a meeting about me. He admitted they were wrong. "Of course you don't need a credit check," he said.

We must have talked for 15 or 20 minutes—quite a lengthy discussion, considering how little I like to talk on the phone. To make a long story short, the next Friday, Lake Erie Bottled Water delivered a cooler with a big bow around it to wish my friend a happy move, and I sent them a copy of my first book.

(Have you read it by now? Did you like it?) The woman in customer service called me and my friend to apologize. Lake Erie Bottled Water has good management. They jumped on the problem right away, the right thing to do.

☑ What Should Be Done?

I love happy endings to frustrating experiences. This owner is trying to do the right thing. I even did a seminar for the company, and we have formed a great relationship. In fact our relationship is so good that I get my water for free.

A company that has 10,000 accounts might have difficulty keeping them all straight. But in my opinion a company like this one really needs to make a serious investment in a good software program.

Software programs can be unbelievably helpful. You can use them to track all sorts of important information, including the customer's orders and payment, their profiles, and their comments.

Also, the owner of a company like this one should form an association with at least one or two other quality companies that are in the same business but that don't compete for customers, for example, a company in another part of the country. The companies could share expertise, software, and so on.

This story had a happy ending because this company has good people who want to give good customer service, and that's what counts.

This episode is a good example of what companies should do, and do more often, especially when problems arise. These employees acted in a proactive mode; they were not reactive or defensive with the customer.

In the months since this experience, I have gotten to know the owner and his family. They are nice, down-to-earth people, trying to run a good, reputable business. They care about their employees, and the employees know it, which means that turnover is reduced and less money and energy is spent on hiring new people.

This company is on the right track, headed in the right direction to be a great company that really stands out.

CONFUSEY FURNITURE LINE

took a big step up from my old beanbag chairs. I bought a new couch, a sectional, that cost about $3,000. About a year and a half later, the back started to wobble. So I called for service.

The retailer I bought the sofa from was no longer in business, and the Confusey line had been taken over by another furniture company. I called them and talked to two people there. They both said, "We're sorry, there's nothing we can do."

So I called Confusey directly. I talked to two people, got voice mail, and went back to the operator, who directed me to Heather in customer service. Heather told me to copy down the serial number, which was on the underside of the couch, and send that and a copy of the original receipt to the company, and they would review my situation and get back to me.

So I got a flashlight and pencil and paper, got down on the floor, crawled under the couch, found the tag, and scribbled down the number. I guess they put the tag in such an impossible spot just so people won't remove it.

This task was just the beginning, and judging by the way they were talking to me on the phone, I expected a customer service nightmare. But the company did keep its word. Customer service called me, and a repairman named Joe came out.

Joe did a good job. In fact, I was so impressed that I called Confusey while he was at my house. I wanted to thank the company because most people don't give accolades—they just call to complain. I asked for Heather, the person I originally talked to. I thanked her and told her everything was perfect. She appreciated the call.

About a week and a half later, I got a call from a second guy, John. He said Heather had told him to call me about rescheduling an appointment to repair my couch.

How my name got into *that* loop, I can't figure out. I just don't know. . . .

☑ What Should Be Done?

This scenario is a bittersweet event, ying and yang, good and bad. On the positive side, I did get my couch fixed. The negative is that I had to do all that work. I had to dig out my receipt (I was surprised that I was able to find it). I had to get down under the couch and find the serial number. And I had a bit of hassle on the phone to get someone to come make the repair.

I can understand a breakdown in communication between two people in a company. But a breakdown in communication when only one person is involved? Didn't Heather ever talk to herself? Even so, if Confusey had had decent record keeping or an efficient computer system for tracking, their people wouldn't have called me to schedule a repair their company had already made.

This type of problem can be easily rectified if management would find the right software program for its customer service people.

One thing I rarely see in companies any more is proactive management. What I mean by proactive management is that the owner or manager actually behaves like a coach, going onto the playing field alongside the players. Confusey's customer service manager should delegate paperwork for a day and go sit next to staff and watch them work.

As coach, you take notes and listen. Then, later in the day, you hold a one-on-one session with that employee and replay what happened and how situations should have been handled.

If you go onto the playing field on a consistent basis, you will improve the skills of your people, and you will have first-hand knowledge of what is happening day to day in your company.

12 Almost Perfect

MY FAVORITE AUTO PEOPLE: MOTORCARS TOYOTA

This great company is one of the many new-car dealers in the **Motorcars Group.** The car I bought is one of the new Toyota Sport Utilities, the RAV 4. It's great, and so is my salesperson. I recommend him wholeheartedly.

It was a quick sale because I knew what I wanted. I needed a reliable vehicle that I can drive under any conditions. I didn't want an expensive car because, with my travel schedule, I leave my vehicle outdoors in an airport parking lot for at least 100 days out of the year, where it's exposed to acid rain and all that other stuff in the air.

Here is the almost perfect part. I picked out the car I wanted and said it would be a cash deal, quick and easy for both parties. After I got delivery, the salesperson said, "We made a mistake. We didn't charge you for the armrest we installed. It will be another $50."

I said, "Hey, I just spent $19,000 for a car, and now you are asking me for another $50. Forget it!" They immediately backed off because they knew I was right.

Now, the positive part, the area in which this company is *perfect,* is in service. I own a number of cars, including a couple pretty exotic ones, but the best service I have ever had in my life is at this Toyota dealership.

First, the service writers couldn't be any nicer. Every time I go into their dealership, they are smiling, they are always nice, and they always remember my name and treat me as if I were their only customer. Even if I drop in unannounced, they fit me into the schedule and treat me with undue respect.

Second, every time I am there, whatever I need is done quickly. Third, my car is always *washed* when I pick it up! And there's more. The last time I was there, the service people also gave me a tube of touch-up paint at no charge. This company is class.

I recently needed a 15,000-mile checkup, which they said would cost about $250.

I said, "Fine, do whatever you want. Just make my car happy."

When they were done, they told me the bill would be lower because my vehicle didn't need something—they told me what, but to me it was technical motor talk. The bill was $160!

Do you think I should trust these people? You bet—for life!

Motorcars Toyota has a terrific manager who provides non-stop training for all employees, whether they are service writers, mechanics, or parts staff. The manager has hired great people with good attitudes who really get a kick out of pleasing the customer.

The formula is simple but effective. If your employees are happy and having fun, so will the customers. (Are you amazed that I am talking about a car dealership? Is yours anything like this?)

This situation can be duplicated in any business—as long as you pay attention to your employees and to your customers!

STOP THE PRESSES! COMPUSA

My first customer service experience with this company was not so good. Back in December 1996, my accountant David, was looking for a computer for his home. We went to CompUSA because it was nearby.

Near the back of the store, two guys were stacking boxes. They had golf shirts on that said "CompUSA," so I figured they worked there.

I said, "Excuse me, I have a couple of questions."

They said, "Yes," but they didn't stop stacking the boxes while they answered my questions. They were actually salespersons, but they wouldn't walk away from the boxes. They didn't even make a move to show us the computer we wanted to see. Do you think we bought there? Not that time!

It's hard to find a great computer store. I had been to this store several times, and during that visit I did not experience good service. Either the manager was having an off day or the district manager was on vacation.

With the right chain of command, the right training, the right attitude, and some basic skills, our experience of poor service could have been rectified to make this store consistently great. A computer store that gives great service all the time would have my undying gratitude and loyalty.

Then, on February 15, 1997, I bought a Monorail computer at CompUSA for $1,299. It killed me to go back there, but no other retailer carried the brand I wanted.

On March 27, I noticed an ad for the same computer for $300 less, that is, for $999. I called CompUSA, even though I could imagine what they would tell me: Sorry, but the 30-day price protection policy has expired. But I took a chance and called them. I would have been thrilled with a $100 due bill, or with anything. Was I surprised.

"No problem," they said. They credited me for the full $300!

Here is a situation of giving someone a second chance. This time the company got it right. They took care of me during the sale, and then they shocked me with great customer service, doing more than I expected, by giving me a refund they *didn't* have to provide.

The 5th Wave   **By Rich Tennant**

©*The 5th Wave by Rich Tennant, Rockport, MA. E-mail: the5wave@tiac.net.*

Yes, now I do go to CompUSA for whatever I need in computer stuff.

ODIE AND THE LIZARD: THE WINKING LIZARD

My friends and I go to the Winking Lizard restaurant quite a bit. It has good food, it's nearby, and it's a fun place. I'm very impressed with it. We did have one unpleasant incident, however.

On this day we had to wait one hour for our food. And we had a waitress with a really bad attitude. She was the kind of person who acts as if getting you a glass of water is a huge favor. With people like this, I'm always afraid that if I say, "When you have a moment," they will take out a Uzi and machine-gun me down on the spot.

Because we had waited so long, the manager came over and told us we would get dessert for free. This offer upset us even more! The people at the next table had been seated after us, and *they* got their meal for free. We thought we should have been given the same deal. We didn't even *want* dessert.

I keep going back to this restaurant because in general it is so good. The Winking Lizard has a busboy named Odie who is one of the nicest, most genuine people I've met anywhere. What's amazing is that every time we go to this restaurant, and we go there a lot, Odie is *always* in a good mood and always smiling. So every time—and I have never done this anywhere else—we tip Odie directly because he is so great.

ALL I WANT IS MY EGG MCMUFFIN: MCDONALD'S

We have to include McDonald's. After all, they have sold billions of hamburgers. I'm doing everything I can to help them get to the day when they have to change all their signs to say "trillions sold." (Needless to say, my doctor is not thrilled by my efforts.)

I decided I was in the mood for an Egg McMuffin. It was about 10:25 A.M., and I thought, "Their drive-through sign says they serve breakfast until 10:30, so I can get there in time."

I was in the drive-in line, and I ordered an Egg McMuffin. No problem. Then I got to the window.

The woman at the window said, "I'm sorry, it's past breakfast time, and we don't serve Egg McMuffins any more." She didn't say, "We've run out of Egg McMuffins," she said, "You can't have it any more."

I said, "Excuse me, I've been waiting in line for seven minutes. You're going to make me an Egg McMuffin. I want one. It's not my fault that I've been waiting in line." I was angry! I said, "I'm not moving my car until you give me an Egg McMuffin!"

Guess what happened. Not only did McDonald's give me *two* Egg McMuffins, they also charged me less.

They said, "We're giving you the manager's price."

I had no idea what they were talking about. Well, the manager's price is a discounted price. The managers at McDonald's knew I was right.

This restaurant is really a great company because, out of all the thousands of times I have been to McDonald's, this incident is the only negative one I can recall ever having.

Let me say one more thing in neon lights, because I can just hear managers saying, "We only pay minimum wage," or whatever they give as an excuse.

McDonald's hires a lot of people at $5 to $7 an hour. If I were hiring employees, and an applicant told me he or she had worked at McDonald's, I would say to myself, "This is a good sign."

I go to McDonald's a zillion times. I think they do a fabulous job.

13

Your Money's Worth: Ingredients of Great Customer Service

In this section I'd like to discuss the concepts and points that I have found to be absolutely essential ingredients of outstanding customer service.

Nonstop Training

All the best companies (see Chapter 14) have done an incredible job of pleasing the customer. This satisfaction is accomplished in only one way: with ongoing training. The key word is *ongoing*. These companies engage in nonstop training.

Picture athletes. In my hometown, our Cleveland Indians have been going great guns. Can you imagine the coach or the general manager going up to the team and saying, "Hey guys, you had a great season. Guess what? Because I'm proud of you and because you have done such a good job, you won't have to practice next year. Here's a schedule of the games. Just show up."

What would happen? The first-place team would end up in the cellar. All professional athletes, in team and individual sports, have professional coaches. All professional athletes practice nonstop.

But when it comes to customer service, we rarely practice. We go to a seminar once or twice a year. I call that deodorant. It wears off, and you smell bad again the next day.

The winning companies have ongoing training that involves everyone. It has to start at the top, with senior management, and continue through all levels of the company. Training also has to continue from day to day, and it has to happen in countless ways.

Every company in the world has an *advertising* budget. I don't care how much it is. It could be as little as a listing in the phone book or a sign on the front door. But most companies do not have a *training* budget.

The Lemonade Stand

What was your first business venture? Let's think back to when you were six years old, and you decided to have a lemonade stand. You needed help, so you got your kid brother or sister and your best friend. You made the lemonade, and you got some paper cups and a stand. You made a sign—your advertising is done. You got the location, and you were in business.

After you sold lemonade for a while, and you were in the hot sun for a few hours, you had to go to the bathroom. What did you do? You got your kid brother, kid sister, or best friend to pinch-hit for you.

Here's where *training* kicks in. Who trained your employees not to drink the profits? Who trained them to ask for a nickel or a dime, and not give the lemonade away?

The better the training, the more lemonade you sold. And if you trained your people to go out proactively and grab customers instead of just sitting quietly behind the stand, sales went up.

What if you wanted to have the lemonade stand open every day? Or if you wanted to open more lemonade stands? Did you just collar more kids and plunk them behind the stand? Or did you train them?

Training is important for every business, not just a lemonade stand. And it's important on an ongoing basis.

Have Fun

That's another key concept. I believe work should be fun. Two people have really changed my life. Most likely you have heard of both of them or read their books.

One is Og Mandino. He was a tremendous person, the truest gentleman I have ever met. Og Mandino passed away on September 3, 1996. He was probably one of the most prolific authors this planet has ever seen. I'm told that about 14 million copies of his books are in print.

Og Mandino has this line in one of his books: "Do you realize that the only creature that has the ability to laugh is man?" I was in Africa on a safari a few years ago, and I can tell you that even laughing hyenas do not laugh. They are predators. They will eat you.

But think about this: We spend two-thirds of our life at work. Of the one-third that's left, we spend about half of *that* third thinking about work. If we aren't having fun while we are working, something is drastically wrong. I think we have to change our attitudes so we really have as much fun as we can, including when we work.

The other person who changed my life is a doctor, Bernie Siegel, the well-known cancer specialist. He has written a number of books and is on the speaking circuit. He has two quotes that I particularly cherish, especially because I am a former cancer patient and a cancer survivor. Here are his two lines:

✔ Life is uncertain. Eat dessert first.
✔ If you can't take it with you, don't go.

I think these lines say a lot.

Also, Bernie Siegel says that after experiencing cancer, patients like myself tend to look at life through a child's eyes. We tend to see every sunrise as the first sunrise, every sunset as the first sunset, every flower as the first flower. Things become more amplified to us. It's important that *all of us* try to keep that vision all the time.

Learn from Children

I think we can learn so many things from children. Here are a couple of lines I have gotten over the years from anonymous authors. I think you might like them:

✔ You can be anything you want to be when you grow up.
✔ Nobody can pedal your bike for you.

165

✔ If you wait until you are really sure, you will never take off your training wheels.

And this one is my favorite:

✔ You have to eat a lot of cereal before you find a free toy. These lines apply as much to adults as to children.

You can be anything you want to be when you grow up— if you go after it. Most people stay stuck in one job or one place. They stagnate. They are afraid to change, to take a chance, to take charge of their lives.

Nobody can pedal your bike for you. If you want to do something, to get somewhere, you have to make it happen.

If you wait until you are really sure, you will never take off your training wheels. There are no guarantees. No risk, no gain.

You have to eat a lot of cereal before you find a free toy. Nobody believes in fun more than I do. But life still requires effort.

It helps to remember all those things that we were told to do when we were kids. We need to continue to do those things. As Robert Fulghum has reminded us in his books: Play fair. Don't hit people. Clean up your own mess. Say you are sorry if you hurt somebody.

These things are very important to a balanced life. I think if we have the right attitude with our life and have fun, our companies will run much better.

Attitude, Attitude

After the 1996 Olympics, I read an article in *USA Today* about the Olympic athletes. They are trained to focus totally on thinking positive and on doing their best.

Think about what most of us do in everyday life. The average human being can think at the speed of about 1,000 words per minute. Studies have shown that fully 70% of our thoughts are negative. That's strong stuff.

The most televised moment of the 1996 Olympics was in the gymnastics team competition, when Kerri Strug made her final vault with a sprained ankle. As she got ready, she wasn't thinking, "Oh, my ankle is hurt. I can't do this." No. She was trained to think, "I will stick this landing. It will happen. It will be my best vault ever. A ten."

If Olympic athletes are trained to think only positive, don't you think people in your company can be trained the same way? Absolutely. It's going to take time, but we can do it. We need more companies that give incredible service.

The Power of Your Mind

This example was given to me by Dr. Richard Fratianne, a physician. I sit on a board of directors with him. Dr. Fratianne is a very intelligent man and the director of the burn unit at MetroHealth, a major medical center in Cleveland.

Here's his story. It involves using your imagination. Keep reading this book, but put it down on your desk or on your lap.

Put your left hand out in front of you and look at it. In your left hand, you are holding a lemon. Now put your right hand out in front of you. In your right hand, you have a knife (unless you are left-handed—then, for safety's sake, switch the knife to your left hand). Cut the lemon in half and put the knife down. In your hand, you have a half a lemon. Now— you really have to do this—take the lemon up to your mouth and bite into it. Close your eyes when you bite into it.

Did you taste a lemon? If you did, and about 50% of the people in our seminars do taste a lemon, think about how powerful your mind is. Look at your hand. There's nothing in it. If you tasted a lemon, you tasted something that wasn't there. That's how powerful your attitude is.

Happy Employees, Happy Customers

A *corporation* is a piece of paper. A *company* is made up of people. If the CEO and the top management of the company have the right attitude and if they really care about their people, all the people in that company will know that and will be happy employees.

And if you have happy employees, you will have happy customers. It all trickles down.

So the idea here is to take care of your employees, treat them with respect, treat them well, and let them have fun. Then they will also have fun with their customers, which means that customers like you and me will be treated properly.

One example I like to use in my seminars is the Scotch brand transparent tape store from *Saturday Night Live* back in the 1970s. Bill Murray and Gilda Radner did this skit. The only thing they sold was Scotch tape. Simple, fun, and a single purpose.

Imagine that your company has only one customer. How would you treat that customer? Like royalty? Why can't you do that with all your customers? Enthusiasm is very important. Make the customer feel important, and help people. Just try always to help people.

Five Steps to Great Customer Service

Here are my points for developing and keeping good business:

1. Answer phones promptly. I don't know about you, but I get upset when I call a company and the phone just keeps ringing and ringing. If I wasn't angry to begin with, I get angry when nobody answers the phone.

2. Return all phone calls. It's rude not to return a call. Even if you don't have an answer, call back and say, "It will be two hours"—or two days or whatever—"before I can give you an answer." If you are the CEO or manager, have your

168

secretary call back. To ignore a phone call is just plain rude—period!

3. Learn to apologize, to say "I'm sorry." Those two words are the biggest words you can say. Also learn to say "I'll find out." Never say just "I don't know." Find out!

4. Try to correct problems quickly. Problems do not go away by themselves. You have to take care of them. As I've already said, a problem is a creative opportunity. It gives you a chance to exceed your customer's expectations and to win that customer *for life!*

5. Get to know your customers. Harvey McKay talked about this strategy in his book *Swim with the Sharks*. The better you know your customer, the better the relationship will be between the two of you.

My company, Direct Opinions, made literally millions of phone calls to customers to determine their level of satisfaction. We asked them three questions that I think every company should use:

1. "Were you (the customer) satisfied with the service?" If you are afraid to ask this question, you shouldn't be in business.

2. "Do you have any suggestions on how we can improve or how we can better serve you?"

3. "Would you return to us or use our company again in the future?"

These are simple questions to ask, but they are very important.

Most companies talk about customer service programs and how to stay in touch with their customers, but in most cases those programs are just a fad—here today, gone tomorrow. The future is with the best companies who take the best care of customers. Virtually all companies are competitive in price, but it's what you really do with your customers, day in and day out, that will make the difference. You have to prove to customers that you really care.

Two Phrases That Say It All

Forget the mission statement. All mission statements say the same thing, and they do absolutely nothing for the customer.

If you and your company can live by these two phrases *and* if you can actually implement them every single day, then you will be providing exceptional customer service.

The first phrase is:

Customer service is doing more than the customer expects.

The second phrase is:

Customer service isn't what you think it is—it's what the customer thinks it is. Customer service is not what you think is important—it's what the customer thinks is important.

Imagine that you own or manage a restaurant. You ask a customer, "How was everything?"

The customer says, "It was terrible."

You say, "How about a free dessert?" Maybe the customer doesn't want dessert, or maybe is on a diet, or maybe is diabetic. If so, free dessert is not what the customer wants. The customer wants great service or to be compensated for poor service, either now, today, or sometime in the future.

Instead, you should simply say, "What would you like us to do for you?" Usually when the question is phrased that way, the customer only wants half of what you expected to give. It's surprising, but if you are not prepared to ask that statement, you have no business dealing with the public.

The Rule of 99

How good does something have to be in order to be good enough? Would you say that a product or service with:

[ ] 75% quality   [ ] 90% quality   [ ] 99% quality
will absolutely be good enough?

If you chose 99%, then you said that 99% quality is good enough and that you are willing to depend on people to do things right 99% of the time. That means you are willing to:

✔ Use unsafe drinking water four days each year.
✔ Go without telephone service for 15 minutes each day.
✔ Go without electricity, water, and heat (or air conditioning) for 15 minutes each day.
✔ Have your heart fail to beat 32,000 times each year.

On a national level, 99% quality means that:

✔ Every hour 16,000 pieces of mail are lost.
✔ Every day two planes make unsafe landings at Chicago's O'Hare airport.
✔ Every week 500 surgical operations are incorrectly performed.
✔ Every year 20,000 drug prescriptions are incorrectly filled.
✔ Every year doctors drop 19,000 newborn babies.

I believe the only acceptable goal is to provide products and services that are right *100%* of the time!

* * * *

You have my permission and encouragement to copy the next page. Enlarge it and put it on the door or wall where you and your people will see it.

The 10 Bullet Points: Hal Becker's Rules for Customer Service

These 10 points sum up the principles of quality customer service. Customer service:

1. Is a commitment and priority coming from top management to do whatever it takes to satisfy the customer.

2. Is the responsibility of everyone—total teamwork.

3. Focuses on what the client wants, not what the company wants.

4. Seeks to develop long-term relationships.

5. Is proactive, seeking customer input and involvement at every phase of the relationship.

6. Means being flexible, not just going by the rules or the computer.

7. Is quality standards, measurements, and performance.

8. Focuses on the positive and on what can be done.

9. Is honest and sincere communication with external and internal customers (employees are internal customers).

10. Is an investment of time and resources that will result in lower costs and improved services.

The best companies in the world have the best customer service programs and spend the most money on training. And—very important—as I said before, the best companies train *on an ongoing basis.*

14 Ten of the Best Companies

Learn from the Masters

The best companies in the world have certain qualities in common. Whatever our business, we all can learn a lot from these companies. Here I have selected the companies that have impressed me most. All have been selected as the best on the basis of my direct personal experience.

Some of these companies are household words. But you don't have to be big and famous to be successful, as you will see from the small companies I have included.

After I selected these ten companies, I called each one and asked some questions about their philosophy and practices in regard to customer service. A few factors really stood out.

First, in virtually every case, when these companies hire new employees, the most important attribute they look for is *a positive attitude*. The critical factor for every company is not a skill or an educational degree, but an aspect of underlying personality that is reflected in behavior.

I don't know of any company that will hire a person without the appropriate attitude and then try to instill that attitude through training. Companies can only reinforce the right attitude with a positive environment, a workplace that's enjoyable to work in. As I said before, a corporation is a piece of paper, but a company is made up of people. And people with great attitudes make great companies.

The second area that really stood out—and this discovery really blew me away—was *the absence of rules*. These companies seem to follow the Nike slogan, "Just do it!" Not one single company had a 100-page policy manual or book of rules. Instead, these companies have ongoing hands-on training to teach their people how to take care of the problems. The employees don't have to worry about making mistakes as long as the customer is satisfied. And this method seems to be working quite well!

The bottom line is this: train people well, empower them to do their jobs, and then let them go and not be afraid to make mistakes as along as they *always, always* put the customer first!

About the Interviews

In putting together this section, I wanted to get more information about these 10 best companies. In my fact-finding mission, I decided to go right to the top in each organization and start with the CEO.

What amazed me was that the higher up I went, the nicer the people were. In many cases, the president referred me down to someone else, typically the public relations department or the vice president of sales, and that was fine. What really impressed me was that everyone returned my calls quickly, without knowing who I was or what I wanted, and they couldn't have been more helpful.

It just shows that the best corporations are run with the best people. It all starts on top with being congenial, talking to people as individuals, and treating them as people. Not one of the people I called was trying to be a big shot.

So, this section was fun to do. You will also find it enjoyable, I think, and we will all learn something.

CALLAWAY GOLF CLUB COMPANY

My friend's mother is an avid golfer. She has a Callaway golf club called Big Bertha. When the shaft broke, she took the golf club to the local retailer from whom she had bought it. The retailer gave her the runaround and didn't have any specific answers.

She figured, "This isn't right. This club is only a year old or so." So she called Callaway directly, asked for customer service, and explained her dilemma. They gave her no problems, no runarounds.

The woman at Callaway immediately said, "We are so sorry. What is the name of the retailer?" She took down the name, and then she told the customer, "Obviously, we can't control our retailers, but we want to make sure that you are happy and that you stay a fan of Callaway golf clubs. We will put a brand-new club in the mail to you. We ask that you put your old club in that box, which will have postage paid for return to us, and send us the old club."

Where do you think this woman will buy golf clubs in the future? Callaway has this customer for life. What a way to run a business!

INTERVIEW WITH CALLAWAY GOLF CLUB COMPANY

Q What is your philosophy regarding customer service?

A I think our philosophy is really just that each time that we encounter a customer, whether it be a retail customer or the end users of our product, we have an opportunity to show them what Callaway is all about, and we want them to leave here with a positive experience.

Q Tell me about your training programs. What do you do, how often, and how in depth do you train? What do you think is important for training new and existing employees?

A We have a training program that runs about two to three weeks, depending on how quickly a new hire goes through the process. Training really is segmented. The first thing that we cover is product knowledge. I feel very strongly that the people we put on the telephone should be the most knowledgeable people in the company about our golf clubs—and from a golfer's perspective, not from an engineer's perspective or a designer's perspective. What does a golfer need to know about this product? Our customer service reps need to know that so that they can communicate with our customers. The second part is that we provide a lot of computer training to our customer service reps so that they can get information quickly and efficiently. That gives them the tools they need to service the customer. The third part is customer service skills. Here we talk about what our policies are, the way we like to approach customers, and the exact type of wording we like to use so that we can be sure that what we say is interpreted the way we mean it. We want to make sure that people have strong communication skills.

Q Do you have a budget for training? Most companies have an advertising budget, but they don't have a clue when it comes to what they spend on training. If you do have a budget for training, how do you drive it? Is it a percent of sales?

A We fall into the no-clue category. We have no idea. We know what we need to do to get people up to speed as customer service reps, and we try to make sure that we do it reasonably in terms of cost. We don't do anything extravagant. We don't send them to Hawaii for their training or anything like that.

Q But you don't have a specific budget set up?

A There is no budget.

Q What do you do to motivate your employees?

A We do a lot of little things. First of all, we compensate our customer service reps very well, probably higher than what you would consider to be the norm. The second thing we do is that we just try to empower people and give them the sense that what they are doing is subject to their own control, and that they should base what they do not only on their own common sense but also on how important

178

the situation is. When we hold meetings with customer service reps, we share success stories that involve customer service. We talk about some exceptional thing that a rep did for a customer—for example, making a 45-minute detour on the way home from work on a Friday night in order to drop a golf club off at the airport, or anything along those lines. We share those types of success stories with all our customer service reps. We share the enthusiasm voiced by our customers about our service. All the letters that we get about our good service are posted around the department. We do those types of things. We also do a lot of little things all the time, like bringing in doughnuts or bagels.

Q What makes you the best in your business? Obviously, it is a really competitive business with new clubs coming out all the time. And what do you think will keep you there?

A Well, from the perspective of customer service, there are two things that make us the best in the industry. First, Callaway has made the commitment that we are allowed to spend the resources, the dollars, necessary to retain customers by keeping them happy. The second thing that makes us the best is the people we hire. We can hire excellent people because we are very competitive in the compensation packages that we can offer to perspective candidates.

Q Nordstrom and Ritz-Carlton have the philosophy that they will do whatever it takes to make the customer happy, and their people are empowered to just do it. Is your philosophy like that?

A Yes, exactly. Our employees are empowered to just do it. That's the most important thing. It is our belief that, from the customer's standpoint, a single point of contact with our company is the most successful way to handle a customer service issue effectively. In other words, customers do not have to talk to the first person and then work their way up the ladder to get a decision made. Also, the person who is making the decision, the customer service rep, does not have to go get approval or sign off to get something done. The customer rep just does it. We tell our reps that if they make a mistake, they should make it in favor of the customer as opposed to in favor of the company, because we are here to keep our customers.

Q That's very much like Ritz-Carlton. What qualities do you look for in potential employees? Can you share any insight on your interviewing process. What questions do you ask?

A First of all we look for a positive attitude, because all we really have over the telephone is the attitude of the people working for us and their communication skills. So we look for a very positive attitude and for effective communication skills. Then we look for work experience; that comes first and foremost over education, but education does definitely play a role in hiring a good candidate. If applicants, for example, have worked in sales, have worked in customer service, they have basically had face time with customers. We want to be sure that we hire people who have experience in the position that we are going to put them in.

Q Last of all, is there anything else you want to mention about your policies regarding customer service?

A Basically, we want the customer to have a positive experience. Our policies are that we want to do whatever is needed within reason and whatever is fair to take care of a customer. First and foremost, what our customer service reps need to do on the telephone is to find out what the caller expects.

Q How do you do that? By asking questions?

A Right. I tell our people all the time that our number one policy is that for every rule that we have, there is an exception to it. The customer service rep needs to know when to break the rule. That means the rep has to use judgment. Until our customer service reps find out what the customer issue is and what expectations the customer comes to us with, we don't know what will satisfy that customer. We could send a customer a free club overnight, we could do all the things in the world, but we still might not satisfy the customer because we haven't really truly found out what that particular person wants. Every customer is an individual. Every customer has individual needs. With some customers we might take 10 days to give them something, and they will think we are the greatest company in the world. The next customer might expect us to do it in two hours. It's very important to identify each customer's hot button.

WALT DISNEY WORLD

Go to Walt Disney World, throw a piece of paper on the ground, and start counting. Before you get to 10, someone will pick it up. Now go to any other amusement park and throw a piece of paper on the ground. You can plant yourself on a bench, go to sleep, and the paper will probably still be there when you get up.

But Disney does things differently. They rely on ongoing training. Disney really takes pride in its people. The people at Disney know that if it's not the Disney way, it's the highway. Employees must conform to Disney rules and regulations.

INTERVIEW WITH WALT DISNEY WORLD

Q What is Disney's philosophy regarding customer service?

A Disney is one of the very few companies that are very detailed in providing equal training to every employee. It doesn't matter what you do or what level job you have. The training is equal whether you are going to work in the barn with the Clydesdale horses, whether you are going to work in wardrobe cleaning 10,000 costumes a day, whether you are going to work on a ride, or whether you are going to work with VIPs. You get the exact same amount of historical training, traditional training, and company philosophy. You spend about a week learning about the company before you even learn about your location. So Disney pays attention to detail. When Michael Eisner came in, he sat down with that same kind of training.

Q How does that relate to Disney's philosophy regarding customer service for the visitors who come into the park?

A People say that Disney goes almost overboard, and I mean that in the nicest way, in terms of the attention of detail that is given to every guest. "Guest" is what Disney calls the customer who comes through the doors. Whether it's a guest's first visit or 100th visit, Disney wants it to be a wonderful experience. Disney trains all cast members to treat all guests in that way. In fact, Disney says in the mission statement that this is the happiest place in the world, whether a person is a guest or an employee. So it's hard to be grumpy at work.

Q Do you know if Walt Disney World has a budget for training, and if so, is it a percent of sales or some other formula?

A No, it doesn't work like that at all. Disney World has what it calls Disney University, which is all internal. You cannot take a class there, but you do get certificates of completion at certain stages of your training, whatever the training deals with, such as traditions training or Disney's approach to quality service or team building. Throughout all an employee's years at Disney World, there are benchmarks for the individual to learn more and more and more. The purpose of the learning may be to help you further your career with Disney or it may be intended to keep you fresh and up, to provide new ways to approach the same situation every day. There are cast members, for example, who have been working in the attractions for 15 years or more, and all those years they have been loading guests on the same ride. Those cast members still have great energy about them. That happens because Disney gives so much attention to detail and to training, and the employees in turn portray that to the guests who come through the doors.

Q Can you give me some examples of what Walt Disney World does to motivate employees?

A First, Disney World has some simple things, such as giving employees free admission to the park. There are a lot of employee benefits. Also, Disney World has great methods of communication with their employees, including an internal newspaper that is driven by the fellow cast members, not by upper management. Disney World is a very grassroots kind of place. For instance, Disney World has a lot of grassroots seminars. The cast members come in and state what they want to know from Michael Eisner or the general manager of a certain theme park. Also, there are ways to motivate employees through rewards for perfect attendance and for excellence, through guest comments and through voting by cast members on which of their peers are outstanding in their department. Disney has little awards that an employee can get throughout a week. Guests can comment on you to fellow employees. Supervisors can drop your name in a box at the end of each day to say that you went far beyond the call of duty. There are little things like that going on throughout the company.

Q   What do you think makes Walt Disney World the best in its industry, and what do you think will keep the company there?

A   Disney World knows its business. Disney World knows that the guests who come through the gate are at the heart of everything. And Disney has some great advantages to build on. Disney has something special that makes Disney World so unique: You can actually touch Mickey Mouse. It is not just some computer out there or some virtual-reality technology. You are touching. Mickey Mouse has a warm and soft side. Disney World also has great history. One man's dream started the whole thing, and you can understand what he went through. Walt Disney was not successful with his first efforts. It is like what we say about Einstein and Edison. They had to make so many attempts to make it succeed. Walt had the same thing. As human beings, we sense that, and we have a different appreciation because Walt didn't just walk in and create this company. He built it from the ground up.

Q   What are some of the qualities Walt Disney World looks for when hiring an employee?

A   There are a number of things. First, a person has to have the stamina and personality to tolerate a long day, because the days are long at Disney World. Personality is a lot of what Disney World looks for. Disney wants people with initiative. Candidates don't always have to have a college education, but Disney World needs to know that a candidate has the desire and ability to help take the company to the next level. It is hard. Disney looks for experience, although the company will hire people right out of college.

   The people who do the hiring at Disney World have the ability to sense whether an applicant wants to learn something from the company and whether that individual is able and eager to help take the company to the next level. You could compare the environment to a sorority or fraternity. Disney's people have an unbridled characteristic of wanting to be part of the organization and wanting to help take it to that next level.

Q What are Walt Disney World's policies regarding customer service?

A Disney is a show. That is what makes it so neat with Disney World's customer service. Everything that guests see from the moment they go through the gate is part of the show. There is a lot that goes on behind the scenes, backstage, that the customer will never see. Employees aren't perfect. Some might smoke, but a customer will never see an employee smoking. Disney knows that employees are human and they will have a bad day, so Disney has an area backstage where employees can go and kick a wall if they are getting frustrated. Disney allows them to do it, to get away from their post. Disney says, "I know you are going to get frustrated doing this, but here, step away from the guests. They don't need to see that. This is their vacation, not yours." Disney World puts things like that in place. Disney creates an environment for guests so that it's always entertainment, no matter where you as a guest look, what you touch, what you see, what you smell. That's part of the Disney quality. Disney gives attention to every detail, from the length of fingernail an employee can wear to the tiniest detail of the costumes to the cleanliness of the parks. Disney makes certain that employees who work in support areas really know the park. To work in marketing, for example, you have to spend a lot of time, as much as a year or even more, in the theme park to get to know that park. That time could be extended if the individual wanted to. That effort is true of a lot of Disney World's professional positions. To continue with the marketing example, the marketing department includes that training in its budget

The 5th Wave

By Rich Tennant

©*The 5th Wave by Rich Tennant, Rockport, MA. E-mail: the5wave@tiac.net.*

because the way to learn about the park is by working in the attractions area. How does it function? What drives the guests to go there? As a result, when that individual starts to work in marketing, he or she has a much better feel.

Q Does Walt Disney World do a lot of cross training?

A Disney World cross trains its people continuously. That has an impact in a number of ways. For example, a marketing person works in the park during peak season. You go put on a costume—it might be the costume of a tour guide or an attendant in an information booth or an employee in the kitchen making hamburgers. Then you go out and be part of the park again. That policy results in a number of really positive things. The first result is that you help the park employees out, especially during busy seasons, and help alleviate the stress that everyone is going through. Another result is that Disney World employees can't be detached, whatever their job: You are part of the park. And when you become part of it, you can experience firsthand what is going on.

JM LANDSCAPING

Here's a little company you have probably never heard of. A couple years ago they did something that floored me.

My house was one of the first built in a new development. So a lot of homes were built around me, with all the dirt that goes with construction and landscaping. I got used to dealing with it because it was inevitable.

One day I received a letter. At first I thought it was junk mail, and I was about to throw it away, but for some reason I read it. It started:

"Dear Home Owner, we would like to take this opportunity to thank you for being so patient with us since we first started our landscape development project for our all-time favorite customers, Tom and Joan Adkins. We fully understand the inconveniences we may have caused neighbors while we were involved in this project over the past several months. To show you our sincere appreciation for your tolerance, please find enclosed a little thank you for putting up with us over the past year."

It was a gift certificate. I thought, "What do I want with a gift certificate for landscaping services?" But before I threw it away, I happened to look at it a bit more closely. It was a $25 gift certificate to Outback Steak House!

Was this action above and beyond my expectations? You bet. If I didn't have a landscaper, would I call them? In a heartbeat. If I were dissatisfied with my own landscaper, would JM be my first choice? Yes.

So I called to thank them for the gift certificate. What they said really surprised me. I was one of the only people to thank them. Is this the kind of world we live in, where hardly anyone says thank you for going above and beyond the call of duty? The guy at JM was a very sincere guy, the kind of person who can go very far if he has the right plan and the right focus, and if he keeps his attitude going in the same direction.

INTERVIEW WITH JM LANDSCAPING

Q What is your philosophy regarding customer service?

A My basic philosophy is that I absolutely want to treat my customers as I would want to be treated. If I start a project for a customer, I expect to stay on that job until it is completed and not be running around at 50 different jobs. It's important that once I have quoted a customer a price, there will be no change in the price. If I run into any problems, they are my problems. I will always try to do something extra for a customer—unless that customer, of course, is a pain in the neck. Most of my clients are great people.

Q How do you make sure you provide great customer service?

A I don't take on a whole heck of a lot of work in a year because I want to be on every job. I feel that if I'm not on every job, then I will lose control.

Q Most of my 10 best companies are big companies. You are a small company, but you do have employees who work with you. Do you do any training, and if so, what do you do?

A My training is basic. My new employees work with me, listen to me, and pay attention to everything. I encourage my employees to attend seminars if they are available or to read publications I have. I try to educate my employees as to the proper botanical name of plant materials.

Q Do you have any budget that you put aside each year for training?

A No, I don't, because this is a very small company. I never have more than five or six employees total.

Q Do you do anything special to motivate your employees in regard to morale, behavior, ethics, and similar things?

A As for the motivational portion of it, I try not to belittle the people who work for me. I try to treat them as equals. But at the same time I let them know that this company is not Burger King: Things have to be done my way. Also, I let my employees know that if I am going to chew them out for something, it will be a one- or two-minute ordeal, and the subject will never be brought up again. Along with this, I never attack my employees on a personal level, so they know that they shouldn't ever take anything personally. It will be strictly job-related. It will be constructive criticism. It will be over in a minute or two, and the employee will never hear another word about it. On the other side of the coin, when employees do a better job than I expected of them, I give them a bonus in their paycheck or even that same day. I do little things to help reward them for work well done.

Q What do you think makes you the best in your business?

A I think what makes this company the best is that I have very high values, very high morals, and very high standards. I expect the same values and morals and standards of my employees. And I want to convey that to my customers.

Q What are the qualities that you look for in a potential employee?

A I look for a good attitude. I believe in attitude. I believe that whether you pay someone $5 an hour or $50 an hour, it boils down to having a good work attitude. If a person accepts constructive criticism well or if a person asks questions where they may be in doubt about something rather than trying to fake it, that all shows a good work attitude. A good work attitude also includes being on time for work, as well as the willingness to work a little bit late, to spend that extra bit of time when we are not done at 5:30 P.M. If we might have to work until 7:00 or 7:30 in the evening, I expect my employees not to complain about it. I just had a situation that made me feel good. Last week I went to a big sports tournament in New York. My employees knew I wanted to be there, and all three volunteered to work last Sunday.

Q Do you have policies regarding customer service? What are they ?

A I definitely have policies about customer service. Anything I do for a customer, and that includes material and labor, I guarantee for three years. I watch for potential problems developing in a landscape. Some plant materials will perish. When you put in 200 to 300 perennials, you are going to lose a few. I try to review a project at least two or three times a week for the first year. If I see a problem in a plant, even though it is not dead yet, I replace that plant immediately. It is my feeling that this policy serves customers in a number of ways. If customers had to replace that plant themselves, it would be an inconvenience in a number of ways. First of all, a customer usually does not know the name of that plant variety. Second, the customer must find a nursery to buy this plant, and then the customer has to go there, spend the money, and take the plant home. It adds up to a pain for the customer, whereas it is easy for us to do.

LEXUS

In all U.S. automotive history, Lexus has the greatest customer loyalty. Even though Lexus franchises began as recently as the late 1980s, more than 70 percent of Lexus customers are staying with Lexus. Why? They have never had service like this before in their life.

Toyota owns Lexus. The least expensive Lexus is only $4,000 more than the most expensive Toyota. That's not a big difference in price, considering the cost of cars today.

When you call a typical car dealership for service, the service writer says, "When would you like to come in?" If you say, "Five days from now," the service writer says, "Would 8:00 A.M. be okay?" You just made an appointment.

Now look at what Lexus does. It trains its people to be proactive. The service writer is likely to say, "Sir, it seems that you have a busy schedule. Would you prefer for us to come to your house or your office, pick up your car, and drop off a car of equal value as a loaner? When your car is ready, we will wash it and deliver it to your garage, and we will pick up the loaner. Would that be okay?"

Wow! This is incredible customer service. The rest of the auto industry is saying, "It won't work." But it *is* working. I bet that next year, and years from now, this policy will still be working if Lexus continues its practices and does not cut back. The other manufacturers *will* have to follow!

Lexus states its covenant this way: "Lexus will enter the most competitive, prestigious automobile race in the world. Over 50 years of Toyota automotive experience has culminated in the creation of Lexus cars. They will be the finest cars ever built. Lexus will win the race because Lexus will do it right from the start. Lexus will have the finest dealer network in the industry. Lexus will treat each customer as we would a guest in our home. If you think you can't, you won't . . . if you think you can, you will! We can . . . we will."

INTERVIEW WITH LEXUS

Q What is your philosophy regarding customer service?

A Well, I can read it off the card that every employee gets. This is what we call the Lexus covenant. It was drawn up in 1987 before the brand went on sale. I'll just take the one line: "We will treat each customer as if they were a guest in our home." This was pretty avant-garde back in 1987. Since then, of course, we have seen this echoed in a lot of companies' mission statements.

Q A lot of mission statements don't walk the talk. They just put the mission out there, but they don't really live it. The only one that I have seen do it like that really is Nordstrom, where they say almost the same thing. Does Lexus live its covenant?

A We try really hard to carry it out. We recognize that we don't always achieve it. Life is not perfect.

Q Don't you have the highest Customer Satisfaction Index— what's known as CSI—in the automotive industry?

A Yes, we do. It's very gratifying, and we do it consistently, too. It is a horse race, and there are some other things that we are doing that are very good. In fact, in all but one year of the division's existence, we have been number one in CSI.

Q I know the gap is being closed. Do you find that you have to reinvent yourself because you have to be out in front again?

A Yes. There is a new initiative called, "Just say yes." It is being developed presently. The focus there is to empower all the dealership associates to make decisions right on the front line and not have to tell the customer, "Well, I have to check with so-and-so first."

Q So your employees can just do it. That's like Ritz-Carlton, where first-line employees can spend $2,000 at any time without authorization in order to satisfy customer needs. Can you tell me more about this initiative?

A We don't have all the details worked out on that. When you are dealing, as in our case, with franchise dealers who are their own businesses, it is not quite as easy as if you owned all the stores and could say, "Here is the way it is going to be."

Q I understand you still have the highest amount of loyalty ever in the history of automotive retailing. Is that true?

A We definitely do lead in the luxury brand. Our brand loyalty hovers between 60 and 65.

Q Wow. That is amazing!

A You know, it is a matter of that old and true axiom that it is 16 times more expensive to go find a new customer than it is to maintain a customer.

Q Don't you think it's too bad that the dealers don't get it, especially when you think about all the money they spend on advertising?

A Well, I hope our dealers get the message. I think they do.

Q I was talking about dealers in general.

A Yes, and we try to drill this into our dealers, that they can maintain the database and things like that. Lexus has a lot of other statements on its philosophy. One talks about treating customers the way they want to be treated.

A That is a slightly different twist on the golden rule.

Q It's my impression that a lot of companies are using Lexus as a benchmark. Is that true?

A Yes, absolutely. Most of the companies that approach us are not in the automotive business. We spend a lot of time fielding requests. We get tons and tons of requests to see our benchmarks. It is interesting because Intel never really viewed themselves as a consumer product. You may remember that they had the Pentium. They finally realized that their customer was the person who used the computer, not the computer manufacturer. The real customer is the end user.

Q Can you tell me a little about your training programs? You are known to be an industry leader when it comes to training the dealer. What do you do that's different?

A Lexus does one thing that really stands out. Every year we hold a national tour, a training ride-and-drive event all over the United States. For this we bring all of our products and our competitors' products and have a two-day seminar. We encourage everyone in the dealership to attend, not just sales people, but everyone, including the lot porter and the cashier and the detailer. Everybody is encouraged to come to the event and drive the cars, to get trained and learn. The national tour that we just completed was a month-long activity; and 75 percent of all dealership employees in the United States participated in it. That was a huge improvement over the previous year. Every year we get more and more people. I think that is unusual because the other sales training programs are for salespeople.

Q But you continue your ongoing training for all employees, don't you?

A Oh, yes. We have a certification program for every level of associate at the dealership. One other thing: In order to reward our dealership associates and to make it possible for them to drive a Lexus, we have a subsidized lease program for anyone who is certified.

Q So, it is a little reward for them?

A Yes. It is a pretty good deal. It makes it very inexpensive for an associate to get behind the wheel of a Lexus. This program extends down to all of our people, at every level of the dealership. The dealer has to participate. Another thing we are trying to do is to increase the professionalism and commitment by making it a career rather than a job.

Lexus doesn't have a lot of good benefit packages like 401(k) and stuff like that. That is partly because we as a manufacturer are prohibited from providing them.

Q What else might you do to motivate the Lexus employees that, again, is transmitted down to the dealers?

A I think that the vehicle lease program I mentioned is an example. It's a deal, and it's a really good start. I think it was really well received. We are looking at ways that we can improve upon financial benefits. We have the usual incentives—trips and things like that—but compared to many others in the industry, we are heavily weighted on customer satisfaction. With a lot of other companies, you know, the emphasis is on sales: Just make your sales, your CSI.

Q What makes Lexus the best in the business, and what do you think will keep you there?

A Lexus has a strong dealer body. We have a strong retailer body. The reason for that is we started with a clean sheet of paper in 1990.

Q And you got to pick the best.

A We got the very best. We got applications from 10,000 dealers. Out of that 10,000, about 1,500 made the first cut. Ultimately, 70 dealers came out of that, so you can see that we really had an opportunity to be very, very selective. The other half of it is strong product, actually the best product, and that makes for a truly dynamite combination. Other car makers may have excellent dealers or may have an excellent product, but they don't have the whole equation.

Q Right. When you look for employees for Lexus, field reps or whatever, what are some of the qualities that you look for?

A Our parent company is Toyota. We are a separate and autonomous division, but we do have people who switch back and forth between the two companies. Toyota overall insists on high education levels and is looking at the long term. I think we look for employees to have the same long-range viewpoint as the company itself. Lexus is a very patient company. It doesn't simply look at what is the bottom line for just the most recent quarter.

Q Does Lexus really have a 250-year business plan?

A Yes. It is unbelievable. There is a plan for the time when the world's oil supply runs out. Lexus really takes an amazingly long view on everything.

Q Do you have any policies regarding customer service?

A We get asked that question a lot. Lexus does not really have a very rigid set of rules. Lexus says, "Do whatever it takes. Satisfy the customer. Do the right thing." There are of course limits to what we can do. There are in some cases customers who make unreasonable requests.

Q Yes, one or two percent. That's standard in any business.

A Unfortunately, at that point, do you just say no?

Q That's right. Goodbye. Go buy an Infiniti. Is that it?

A Yes.

Q Are your people really free to satisfy the customer?

A Lexus doesn't have a manual that gives its people a flow-chart that says, "If X happens, do this."

Q I am not surprised, because the best corporations say it all on just one sheet of paper: "Just do it."

A Yes, that is basically it. Customer satisfaction begins with our people who work the 800 numbers. They are very thoroughly trained, and then they are allowed to use their own judgment, to make their own calls on what to do.

Q Great. Then they are allowed, they are truly, truly empowered? You don't just *say* they are empowered?

A That's right.

Q And if they make a mistake, or if they do something that is wrong, you don't jump on them for doing it wrong?

A No. Actually, we almost congratulate them. I do believe, from my observation, that erring on the side of overdoing it is generally welcomed because we can say, "Well, nobody can have any doubt that we tried."

Q Your philosophy is to do more than the customer expects.

A Right. I often get requests from companies that say, "Send us your manual." Well, the manual is this little card that sits in my wallet. I'll send you one. That is the Lexus manual.

INTERVIEW WITH A LEXUS NEW CAR DEALERSHIP

Q What is your philosophy regarding customer service?

A The customer is always right.

Q Whoa! That's all?

A The customer is always right, no matter what.

Q What if you get a customer who's a jerk?

A We still try to take the customer at his or her word.

Q Tell me a little about the training programs that Lexus provides for your people.

A Lexus provides us with training in all areas, from answering the phone to sales training to product knowledge and technical knowledge and ride-and-drive competitive models. Lexus is great in that respect.

Q You have been in the business a long time. Do you find that these programs are different from those of the other manufacturers you worked with?

A Our programs are far more in-depth and are conducted much more frequently. It's ongoing. Lexus is always training.

Q So, it is not just stop and hit them when things are bad?

A No.

Q Most businesses, especially in the car business, have a budget for advertising, so you might know what you are going to spend next year. Do you or Lexus have a budget for training?

A Lexus does. I am sure they do. I don't know what that budget might be, but training is very important to them, and it is to us also. We just had an introduction to the new product that is coming out next month, the GS-300 and -400, and we sent 25 people to Chicago for the training and for the ride-and-drive. We sent that many people because our dealership has made a commitment to make that level of training available, but a lot of dealers possibly might not want to send the whole store.

Q What do you do to motivate your employees?

A We secure their jobs. We let them work here. We have virtually no turnover. One person moved out of the state. Basically, we have applications all the time from people who would like to work for us.

Q What makes Lexus the best in the business, and what do you think will keep you there?

A Well, I think it is the philosophy behind Lexus. They set out to build the best products in the world and to get the best dealers in the world to sell their products. Along with that goes the Lexus philosophy that we are to treat the customer like a guest in our home.

Those of us who have done that have been very successful. Lexus builds great products, and the company is continually striving for improvement in all respects: in products, in service, and in training.

Q I am sure Lexus tells its dealers what qualities to look for when you are hiring employees. Are there certain things you are looking for?

A We are looking for professional people who have the "we care" attitude, people who are concerned about people and who are not in it just to make a buck for themselves.

Q Every single top company chairperson, from Nordstrom to Southwest Airlines, says the same thing: attitude. Tell me about your policies regarding customer service. What policies do you have in place?

A We go the extra yard. This is not a Lexus requirement. We provide total valet service. We pick up the customer's car, we leave them a loaner car, and we return their car. Most Lexus dealers just have loaners available. Some of them do what we do, and more of them are starting to. We also have authority from Lexus to do whatever we have to do to make our customers happy. That's part of the Lexus commitment to provide special care and customer satisfaction. We get all the support we need from the factory.

Q Are they a great partnership for you?

A It is a wonderful partnership.

L.L. BEAN

One of the finest mail-order companies in the world today, if not the finest, is L.L. Bean. Many corporations have used L.L. Bean for benchmarking: They have visited L.L. Bean to learn about the kind of systems it has in place, from hardware to software to telemarketing.

When you call L.L. Bean, I defy you to find someone who is nasty. You will always find their people upbeat and enthusiastic. Do they have training? Of course they do, and it's nonstop.

L.L. Bean does not actually manufacture all its products. They have everything manufactured for them by other companies around the world, and then L.L. Bean puts its label on the product. L.L. Bean doesn't even own a truck. They ship everything UPS or Federal Express. But L.L. Bean is still number one in customer satisfaction.

For example, imagine that I bought a shirt from them two years ago. Now I call them and say, "My shirt sleeve has a thread hanging from it."

They say, "Mr. Becker, how long have you owned the shirt?"

I say, "About two and a half years."

With no questions asked, their person asks me to send it back and it will be replaced. L.L. Bean will do everything they can to make customers happy, and that's why they are number one.

L.L. Bean was founded in 1912 by Leon Leonwood Bean (now you know what those initials stand for). Leon opened his first store in 1917 in Freeport, Maine. The store that occupies that site today is open 24 hours a day, 365 days a year, and it draws more than 3.5 million visitors each year.

L.L. Bean's customer satisfaction department also operates 24 hours a day, 365 days a year. The company receives 14 million toll-free catalog and customer service calls in a year. Telephone orders account for more than 80 percent of all L.L. Bean orders; with mail orders, of course, accounting for the other 20 percent. Annually more than 12 million packages are shipped to customers. All incoming and outgoing packages are processed through the order fulfillment center.

During L.L. Bean's busiest week, more than 1 million calls are received. More than 179,000 of those calls come in on the busiest day alone, and about 154,000 packages are shipped on the busiest day in the order fulfillment department. Those days happened to be December 9 and December 17 in 1996, which shows you that a lot of people wait until the last minute to do their Christmas shopping!

During the peak holiday season, L.L. Bean employs more than 8,000 employees, of whom 2,500 are telephone representatives and 2,600 work at the order fulfillment center. At other times of the year, the number of employees totals some 3,500.

L.L. Bean enjoys annual net sales of more than $1 billion. Of that total, catalog sales account for more than $900 million. The company produces about 24 different catalogs yearly and distributes some 115 million catalogs throughout the United States and internationally. L.L. Bean stocks more than 16,000 items, the great majority of them carrying the familiar L.L. Bean label.

The company introduced its Web site in 1995 and offered on-line commerce in 1996. So L.L. Bean is adapting and preparing for the future in addition to being focused on outstanding customer service in other respects.

INTERVIEW WITH L.L. BEAN

Q What is your philosophy regarding customer service?

A In the past, our philosophy was that we wanted to treat the customer the way we wanted to be treated, but we have changed our philosophy a bit. What we say now is that we want to treat the customer the way the customer wants to be treated.

Q Ooh. Tony Alessandra, in his book *The Platinum Rule,* says exactly what you said, treat the people . . .

A Yes. We do stress to our reps that they are not here to match wits with the customer. The customer is right. The customer may have a situation where we can help educate them, but in their mind's eye, they are right regarding whatever they are asking for.

Q Great. Can you tell me about your training programs? What do you do, and how often?

A We give a full week of training to all of our new hires, the people we bring into the company. Our training covers the

systems that they will be using, the communications that
we will be expecting, and the please and thank you—
those important courtesy phrases.

Q What do you have for existing employees? How often? Is it
ongoing?

A We give training once a month. Actually, we have what we
call a team day. It's a day in which they learn about the
business, and it can be anything from a business update to
training on new products that are coming out.

Q Every company has an advertising budget. But I find that
when I ask the company about its training budget, they
don't have an answer. Does your company have a training
budget? If so, is it set in stone, such as a percent of sales?
Do you have a budget set aside for training?

A Yes, we do.

Q Great. We'll leave it at that. What do you do to motivate
employees? How do you keep morale high, and all the rest?

A Well, one of the things we try to do is to catch people doing things right.

Q That goes along with what Ken Blanchard says. Don't always look at just the things that are wrong.

A On our team meeting days, we will stand up and read customer compliments or things that an employee's peers said
about them. That gives a wide audience the benefit of
knowing what their fellow workers are doing, and it gives
our employees public recognition.

Q What makes you the best in your business? What do you
think will keep you there?

A I think it is our customer service.

Q And you just try to improve constantly on what you are doing?

A Exactly.

Q What are the qualities that you look for from a potential
employee? Is there any one thing first and foremost that
you really look for?

A Most of all, we look for enthusiasm, good work ethics, attitude, and that type of thing. We can teach people and train them on the systems they will be using, but what people bring with them, the motivation within, is very helpful.

Q It's amazing that all the best companies say the exact same thing.

A Yes.

Q Can you tell me anything about your policies regarding customer service?

A Well, we have a 100-percent guarantee, and that has stood us in good stead over the years. We guarantee the life of the product, and that is deemed in the eyes of the beholder, in the eyes of the customer. They can return it to us.

Q Regardless. Actually, I do have one other question. I've always heard that L.L. Bean is a benchmark company. Your telemarketing and your hardware and software are supposed to be incredible. Without talking about trade secrets, is there anything unique about what you have that makes you so different from everybody else?

A I think we just have a really creative bunch of folks, right from the line employees all the way up to senior leadership. A lot of what we do is home grown. Occasionally we will use consultants who come in and give us some expertise, but a lot of what we do is just good stuff right from within.

MCKEE FOODS

First of all, let me say that all my life I have been a lover of what those spoilsport dentists and dietitians refer to as junk food. My very favorite treat has always been Little Debbie snack cakes. A while ago, while I was doing one of my seminars, I told the group, "I have a confession to make. I'm in love with Little Debbie." Well, there were people from McKee Foods Corporation in the audience, and as a result of that comment I got to know the senior management and do some work for McKee Foods. I got to see the business side of McKee, which I think is every bit as great as their Little Debbie snack cakes. And I got to meet Little Debbie herself!

McKee Foods Corporation is best known for its Little Debbie snack cakes. Annual sales are some $770 million. The company was formed in 1934 when O. D. McKee and his wife, Ruth, bought a small bakery in Chattanooga, Tennessee. In 1957 the business moved to Collegedale, Tennessee. After many expansions of their one location, the McKees gradually added three more plants, in Tennessee, Arkansas, and Virginia.

McKee has paid a lot of attention to its guiding values. They are stated as follows:

People To recognize the value and contribution of each individual, and to demonstrate concern for the health, safety, and well-being of employees and their families.

Integrity To conduct business ethically, honestly, and fairly, and treat everyone with respect.

Responsibility To accept responsibility for our actions and act responsibly in our jobs and in our dealings with each other, our customers, and our communities.

Quality To satisfy our customers with quality products and services, while providing the highest value.

Productivity To maximize the use of our resources to maintain profitability and to support continued growth.

Innovation To use creativity, teamwork, and continuous improvement to "find a better way."

In its company philosophy, McKee stresses a number of values to its employees:

✔ Be honest with everyone.

✔ Be willing to change in order to grow. (McKee has changed its main product and introduced products that are not baked.)

✔ Value your customers. (McKee says, "We wouldn't *be* if they didn't buy. We produce a wide range of products to please a wide range of people.")

✔ Be demanding of yourself and others. (O. D. McKee said, "I'd never ask someone to do something I wouldn't do myself.")

✔ Find opportunities. (The original bakery the McKees bought had been on the market for some time.)

✔ Fill a niche. (McKee's niche is a quality product at a reasonable price.)

✔ Treat people right. (McKee has a long tradition of concern for its employees' safety and well-being.)

✔ Be confident in your abilities.

✔ Don't be discouraged by setbacks. (Turn them into opportunities.)

✔ Take reasonable risks. (Each of the plant's moves was a risk.)

✔ Be ethical.

✔ Find a better way. (McKee has constantly modified or invented machinery and processes and developed new products.)

INTERVIEW WITH MCKEE FOODS

Q What is McKee's philosophy regarding customer service?

A We value our customers. We know that there is such a thing as customer loyalty. A lot of the calls that our customer service department receives are positive calls from people who say either, "I love your product, and I just wanted to let you know," or "I love your products, and I

205

can't find my favorite one in my store." We get letters all the time from people who tell us, "I grew up eating McKee Foods."

Q If they can't find a product in their store, what do you do?

A In our sales department we have someone who calls the retailers and the independent distributor to find out why that product is not in that customer's store.

Q Tell me about your training programs.

A We do on-the-job training and quality training for everyone, from the people who operate our lift trucks and our wrapper machines all the way up through management.

Q And it is ongoing, I take it?

A It is ongoing. It is constant. McKee is in the process of setting up a learning center at one of our plants. We have three plants locally, and they are all located close together, but one of them has started something called the learning center. It has all kinds of learning materials available for employees, and they can go at their own pace with reading, math, and dozens of other programs.

Q How is McKee's training budget set?

A I don't know how that's done. I have a feeling that it is like my budget, and it is set as a percent of sales.

Q But McKee does have a budget?

A Absolutely.

Q Beautiful. What do you do to motivate your employees?

A I think profit sharing is a big motivator. Employees know that if they cut waste and if they come up with new ways of doing things—what we call a better way—it will result in more profits, and those profits will be shared in September. When employees have been with McKee for two years, they start to receive a profit-sharing check, and a similar amount goes into their retirement fund, where it grows and grows. We also have a 401(k) plan. That can really add up.

Q I understand that at McKee the results of profit sharing can really be substantial.

A Well, last year the growth in my retirement fund was greater than my income. There is a big value in that. It reduces turnover. I think it is a big motivator, which is why Elsworth McKee started profit sharing in the first place. When he was a young man working in the company, bonuses were given just to the people in top management. Elsworth McKee felt that was not fair because any profit realized by the company happens to a large extent as a result of all the people who work every day on the line, and they should share in the profit, too. So, profit sharing has been going ever since McKee introduced it about 40 years ago, and every year since then has been profitable. Before profit sharing, McKee was up some years, down some years.

Q What makes you the best in your industry, and what do you think you will do to keep McKee there?

A The company is very conservatively run. I'm talking in terms of practicing economy. For example, when the company bought an airplane for business travel, they immediately redid the whole interior of that plane so they can put more people in there. They even removed the bathroom, the luxurious one, and replaced it with a seat with doors around it that you just pull shut. I have never known anyone to use it because everyone always says, "I'm not going to drink anything! I'm not going to use that bathroom!" You will never see the McKees throwing their golf clubs into that plane and going away for a weekend in Florida. It never happens.

Q That's quite a story. It sets quite an example.

A The people who have been promoted to top positions are very conservative fiscally. And I think the reason why this company became successful was that the founders, Odie and Ruth McKee, were absolutely the perfect couple for this. Odie was the entrepreneur and the risk taker, the person who wanted the best of everything, and he wanted it right away. Ruth was the one who was cautious with money and wanted to know there was going to be a paycheck, and she made sure that Odie kept his feet on the ground. That was a really good combination. Either one of them could not have done it without the other. The one would have put us in the hole, and the other one would not have taken the necessary risks. I think that the people in top positions at McKee today continue to be that kind of a mix of people. Some of them are risk takers, and some are conservative. We have carried on that tradition.

Q Does McKee have any policies regarding customer service?

A People have tremendous latitude. An individual who heads a department can pretty much run the department as if it were his or her own business. When there's a customer service problem, the individual has the latitude to do whatever it takes to make the customer happy. It may involve taking the work away from an employee who is not giving the customer good service and giving it to somebody else who will.

MUELLER TIRE

Mueller Tire, located in Cleveland, Ohio, is a chain of retail tire stores that sell different manufacturers' tires and that provide services such as wheel alignments and oil changes. One of its two owners, Scott Mueller, has taken service to a whole new level. And whatever it takes to make a customer happy, Mueller will do it. The company is nationally recognized for its incredible customer service, especially its money-back guarantees and its own tire warranty program.

If Mueller Tire finds a nail when rotating your tires, they fix the tire for free. If you get an oil change, Mueller gives you a free tire rotation. They don't oversell. They ask a lot of questions to find out what you need, and that's what they sell you—nothing more.

Counter staff, installers, and other employees are trained in customer-service techniques at what is called Mueller University. Most of these techniques have been around since Noah's time—but Mueller trains its people to be enthusiastic and to continually do everything they can to make the customer happy.

It starts with hiring. Mueller has taken the time and effort to choose the right people to fit its company profile. Mueller runs its operation with the attitude "Put the customer first, and do whatever it takes to please the customer."

INTERVIEW WITH MUELLER TIRE

Q What is your philosophy regarding customer service?

A I guess it boils down to two things. One, we realize that we are in the "need" business as opposed to the "want" business. When customers come to us, they need to have something done to their car. They do not particularly want to be here. They have to be here. We ultimately believe that our mission and our company are formed around the goal of making the whole experience hassle free. Put another way, our goal is to make a basically unpleasant experience pleasant. That is really one of the core things that we try to keep focused on. That is our mission, to be a hassle-free provider. The second important thing in our philosophy is that we view our customers over a long-term period, not a short-term one. We try to develop a customer as a client for life. This way we maximize the revenue and profit by looking at the whole lifetime relationship with a client as opposed to a single, one-time sale. I think that when you take this approach you do things a lot differently. It affects how you price your products, what your warranty policy is, and so on. It really meshes with our philosophy and mission of providing a hassle-free experience. We really treat our customers as long-term friends and develop a strategy to support that. Another thing is that we realize there is only one way we can build good customer service, and that is by building a system that really rewards our associates. A company can have the cleverest marketing in the world, can have the neatest and best locations, and can even have great pricing, but if a company sets out ultimately to provide good customer service, especially in our business, the only way to achieve that is with great associates. Our company is built on a three-pronged foundation. We believe that without unbelievable customer service and satisfaction, we are not going to win as a company. The only way to get there is to have great associates. So, they have to be part of the winning equation. A company has to have pay systems or reward systems that enable the company to attract and retain great associates. If you have those things in place, then the customer wins, and that means the company wins.

Q Tell me a little bit about your training programs. What do you do? How often? What do you cover? Do you have programs for both new and existing employees?

A Our goal for a new retail associate is for that person to go through a training process that lasts about a month and that covers everything from A to Z. It includes product training, sales training, and the company mission and culture. Right now, we are actually working to put in place seminars about four hours in length for each new associate that we hire, all our sales personnel, explaining our company's culture and mission in terms of customer service. Basically, it is sales training and product knowledge training. In our industry the typical training takes about one day and is something the employee does on an individual basis. We really take the time to train our people up front. Then, more importantly, because we reward our associates, we have very low turnover. We are continually training our people, even our long-term associates. This year we did a five-month leadership organizational-type training for all our sales associates. We are constantly doing training on product testing and product knowledge. When you invest in people and their training, especially your long-term associates, it is even more rewarding. They have covered the basics, so then you can really take those individuals to the next level. We believe in training, in putting our money where our mouth is. We believe in doing it during the day, when people are alert. When we started out with training, we tried to do the usual kind of approach of holding the session at six o'clock, bringing in pizza, and so on. We soon realized that it's necessary to make the investment in people during the day. We have to pay them for those hours of training, and we realized it's important to train our people when they are awake and effective and their minds can think.

Q Do you have a set budget for training? I'm not asking for the dollar amount. Is it something like a percent of sales, or how do you set the figure?

A Basically, we look at it as a percent of sales. It boils down to spending about $2,000 a year per associate on training, more or less.

Q What do you do to motivate your employees? Are there certain things that you believe in?

A Well, we think compensation is a big factor, but if you can tie compensation to your mission, it becomes a pretty powerful motivator. All our pay systems are set up to pay people double what the industry average is. But on a cost-per-sales-associate basis, our people are actually more efficient than the industry average. We do that just by creating great systems. Every associate in our company is paid according to what our customers think. We do surveys of every customer, and we link that back into our associates' compensation. Every reward we offer and contest we hold focuses basically on the same thing: our customers and our customer service. We have done all kinds of rewards and contests. We have everything from pizza parties to trips to renting a dunk tank. We are constantly trying to do the fun things but at the same time we are constantly focusing on our customers.

Q What makes you the best in the business, and what do you think will keep you there?

A Well, I think it is our dedication and our core ideology. If you are striving to improve and to focus on the customer, you are constantly challenging yourself. You have a core ideology that has brought you to that point, being the best, but part of that core ideology is improving and getting better and becoming more and more hassle free. So I think that when you look at what has gotten us there, what has made us the best, and what is going to keep us there, you're going to see one thing: just constantly focusing on the customer and being relentless, not resting on our laurels. There is a friction. We do some things right, but we are constantly challenging ourselves to become a better company and even more hassle free. We are constantly re-examining what we do. We never change our core ideology, but we are always looking at all of our systems and procedures. We reexamine those so we can continually improve.

Q What are the most important qualities that you look for in a potential employee?

A Well, we look for three things basically. Our people must work hard, be nice, and love cars.

Q Do you have any basic policies regarding customer service?

A We have pretty broad policies. You could sum it up by saying that the bottom line is to make the customer happy at all costs. We tell our employees that when in doubt, they should always err on behalf of the customer.

We believe in the basic fairness of our customers. We tell our employees, "Occasionally, people will try to cheat you, but for the most part, you assume that the customer is being fair and you should really treat them fairly." We tell our people to do whatever it takes to make the customer happy.

NORDSTROM

Almost everyone is familiar with the legendary service provided by Nordstrom department stores. What really impresses me is that Nordstrom doesn't advertise its legendary service. Nordstrom service is legendary precisely because Nordstrom actually puts into practice the company policy of providing customer satisfaction *all* the time. Here are two examples that really tell the story. I heard these from people I have met at my seminars.

A man walking through Nordstrom saw a pair of shoes he liked. He said to a clerk, "Do you have these shoes in 9 medium?"

The clerk said, "Let me go check." He came back and said, "Sir, I'm sorry. We are out of stock. Can you come back in ten minutes?"

When the customer came back, he was greeted by the clerk, who was beaming and excited.

The clerk said, "Sir, I got your shoes!"

The customer thought, "So, big deal. That's your job." When the clerk handed him the box, the customer said, "Wait a minute. This box is from your competitor."

The clerk said, "Yes, I know. We were out of stock, so I went into the mall and bought the shoes from our competitor."

The customer said, "You went and bought shoes from your competitor? Doesn't Nordstrom have these shoes on sale for $10 less?"

The clerk said, "Oh yes, you pay our sale price. That $10 comes out of my pocket, but Nordstrom will reimburse me for the rest."

The customer said, "Wait a minute! You went down to the mall, bought the shoes from a competitor, pay the $10 difference out of your pocket, and Nordstrom reimburses you? Why didn't you just send me down to the mall?"

The clerk said, "Sir, I want you as *my* customer."

Don't you think that for $10 this clerk has gained a customer for life? I think so.

Here's another example: A woman walked into Nordstrom with an automobile tire and said, "My tire blew up prematurely."

The clerk said, "No problem, do you have your receipt with you?"

The customer said, "No, I don't."

The clerk said, "Do you know how much you paid for the tire?"

The customer said, "About $80."

The clerk said, "Do you have an account with us?"

The customer said, "Oh, yes, absolutely."

The clerk called up some information on the computer, saw that the woman had a Nordstrom account, and said, "No problem, we can take the tire back."

The clerk may have had to make one phone call to a supervisor to get an okay, but it was done on the spot. The woman's account was credited for $80.

Now for the punch line: Nordstrom doesn't even *have* a tire department. But they wanted to satisfy a customer. They know how much it costs to bring a customer into the store, and they know how much will it cost to have that customer never come back. They know that a lost customer will cost them a lot more than $80.

Here's a fact: the average retail department store does approximately $158 in sales per square foot. Now here's an amazing fact: Nordstrom does $383 in sales per square foot. Does their service pay off? Of course!

Ready for another impressive fact? I found that the average retailer spends about 8% of its budget on advertising, while Nordstrom spends only about 2% of its budget on advertising.

Nordstrom buyers operate like entrepreneurs. (Nordstrom's business, by the way, is roughly 80% women's clothing and shoes.) The buyers choose merchandise to suit the taste of the shoppers at that individual store rather according to a single policy for the entire company.

Nordstrom's sales clerks have the authority to accept or reject returns, to honor gift certificates, and to exchange merchandise. With that independence come rewards.

Including base pay and commissions, the average full-time salesperson makes about $29,000, more than double the national average. Most salespeople can make a 6.75% commission, but in a few departments, such as shoes, they can make

10% Serving customers well can be very profitable for sales-people. A few top salespeople make as much as $100,000 annually from serving their customers.

The employee handbook consists simply of a single piece of index paper, just 5 inches by 8 inches. The wording on it welcomes employees and ends with this sentence: "We only have one rule." On the back of this sheet of paper, in large letters, is just this one sentence: "Our only rule: use good judgment in all situations."

INTERVIEW WITH NORDSTROM

Q What is your philosophy regarding customer service?

A Our philosophy regarding customer service is to treat every person who walks in our doors as if we are welcoming them into our own home.

Q It's a nice house! A real nice house!

A Thank you. Our philosophy is to treat people with respect, to listen to our customers, and to try to satisfy their needs. Also, I would like to go a little further than that. Our goal, what we have set ourselves up to try to do every day, is to satisfy the customer. Now, we know that we are not always able to achieve that. We try to create an environment that allows our people to do that. One of the ways we do that is by empowering our people to take care of the customer. We set our people free. We give them no rules.

Q But you truly empower them so that they can do it? It is not just a buzzword?

A Right. Our employee handbook—you must have heard about this before—is one piece of paper. It says that there is one rule at Nordstrom, and the rule is to use your good judgment at all times.

Q I've heard that Nordstrom expects its people in management to function as coaches.

A That's right. We are coaches to our people, and as coaches our job is to help keep them using their best judgment at all times. There are times when people may not use their best judgment, and when that happens, we are going to let a customer down. We think there are a lot of people out there in America who want jobs that enable them to feel empowered to take care of customers the way customers should be taken care of. It is not that hard for us to find good people because we go out and say to people that Nordstrom has an environment where we are going to say to you, "Take care of the customer the way you think the customer needs to be taken care of." If you do that, you are going to be successful.

Q When you opened the Nordstrom in Cleveland, you didn't bring in a lot of magical people. You just took people who came to you from other stores, and said, "Now we are going to let you do the right things."

A Right. And we also had to teach the 450 people we hired a few things.

Q That leads right to my next question. Tell me a little about your training programs. Are they ongoing forever?

A Yes. We have very little formalized training. We have one day of training on the register and one day of company orientation. So, we have two days of initial training when a new employee comes in the door. From then on, really, the training is primarily done on the job.

Q So, your managers are really full-time coaches then?

A Yes.

Q Do you have a budget for training? I don't care about the specific dollar amount. Another thing is that I have read that the average retailer spends 8% of its sales on advertising, but Nordstrom spends only 2%. Do you have certain money set aside for training?

A Well, obviously, there is certain money that is committed to the register training and orientation. We have a labor cost there. We don't have, for instance, a training director for the company.

Q That's unbelievable. Are you saying that the best company in the world doesn't have a training director?

A No. All of us are trainers and coaches all the time.

Q Wow! What do you do to motivate your employees in terms of morale and so forth?

A We do a lot of things. For our sales people, the best motivation is our commission pay system. Beyond commission, we think employees like to be rewarded among their peers on a regular basis. At our store meetings we recognize people in front of their peers for giving exceptional service.

Q So you have in-store meetings that are ongoing?

A Yes. We also have award programs for productivity on a yearly basis for people who achieve a certain goal. That's called our pay center club. The highest honor anyone can achieve at Nordstrom is our all-star award. Each month one person from each store is selected and honored for delivering outstanding service on a consistent basis. That happens every month in every Nordstrom store.

Q What makes you the best in your business, and what do you think will keep you there?

A Our people, absolutely. Each day our reputation is enhanced or lessened by the actions of our people. We are only as good as the last customer we served.

Q What is the most important quality you look for when you are hiring new employees?

A It sounds simple, but we look for nice, professional people who enjoy helping people.

Q So, attitude plays a big role here?

A Attitude is a very difficult word to use because it's very ambiguous. We talk instead about nice. That is a really simple word, and it is underused these days. "Nice" really speaks to the kind of people we want to hire at Nordstrom. There are a lot of nice people in the world, and there are different ways to be nice. There is not one correct way, in our opinion, to service every customer. We don't necessarily look for X, Y, and Z in a potential employee because A, B, and C could be just as effective.

Q Can you tell me about your policies regarding customer service. Do you have any policies?

A No.

Q You tell your people to just do it?

A Right. We don't have any customer service policy. Again, that speaks to Nordstrom's whole culture of not wanting to put too many rules in place. If there is a policy, then somebody might say, "Well, I can live up to this policy, but then what if a situation arises where I need to go beyond that? Well, I can't because Nordstrom has this policy." We want people to exceed even our expectations as a company. We want people to find new ways to take care of a customer.

RITZ-CARLTON HOTELS

This is one of my favorite companies. Most people don't realize it, but Ritz-Carlton Hotels are wholly owned by a management company, not franchised like other hotels.

Ritz-Carlton has taken customer service to a whole different level. What makes them so great? Every employee must carry a credo card, a little plastic card that includes their motto: "We are ladies and gentlemen, serving ladies and gentlemen." If you

219

want to be treated like a gentleman, act like a gentleman. If you want to be treated like a doormat, act like a doormat.

Ritz-Carlton has 20 basics that are part of its program of customer service. In fact, the employee entrance of some Ritz-Carlton Hotels has these 20 basics hanging from blue signs, so employees see them every day and are more likely to remember to do the right things. These 20 basics are also printed on the little plastic cards that employees carry.

Of all the 20 basics, my favorite is number 8. It states: "Any employee who receives a customer complaint owns the complaint."

Now, is that empowerment? Absolutely. The Ritz-Carlton takes empowerment to a whole new level. First-line people, such as housekeepers and busboys, have the authority to spend up to $2,000 at any time to satisfy a customer's needs. Managers have the authority to spend $5,000.

That seems like a lot of money. It also involves time, because it takes ongoing training to instill this policy into the employees and to make it daily practice.

What happens? The customer is taken care of. The customer doesn't have to hear, "I can't do that" or "You have to see my manager." The customer doesn't have to fight through the whole chain of command. Something else important happens. The employee feels great, because he or she handled the situation on the spot. So both parties win.

Customers get what they want. And Ritz-Carlton executives say each loyal guest will spend $100,000 in his or her lifetime with Ritz-Carlton.

The Ritz-Carlton Basics

I am totally impressed by what Ritz-Carlton calls its basics. They result in such outstanding customer service that I believe it's worth summarizing the basics here and commenting on some of them. There are 20 basics in all, and every employee is expected to practice them constantly. Specifically, every employee is expected:

1. To know, own, and energize the credo (printed on the employee wallet card; highly personalized customer satisfaction is known to be the Ritz's highest priority and every employee's job; employees understand the need to anticipate and meet customer wishes and the crucial importance of the staff's many daily interactions with customers).

2. To practice the Ritz-Carlton motto, "We are ladies and gentlemen serving ladies and gentlemen" and to practice teamwork and "lateral service" (to internal customers or other employees) to create a positive work environment.

3. To practice the three steps of service (printed on one side of employee wallet card; the hotels know the likes and dislikes of repeat customers, all the way down to the color of ink they prefer in their pens).

4. To successfully complete training certification to ensure that he or she understands how to perform to hotel standards on the job.

5. To understand his or her work area and the hotel's goals as established in its strategic plan.

6. To know the needs of internal and external customers so products and services can be delivered as expected.

7. To continuously identify defects throughout the hotel.

8. To own a customer's complaint (to quote the card: "Any employee who receives a customer complaint owns the complaint").

9. To pacify the customer instantly. This basic includes reacting to correct the problem immediately; and following up with a phone call within 20 minutes to verify that the problem has been resolved to the customer's satisfaction.

Employees are expected to do everything possibly to never lose a guest. (Any manager can spend up to $5,000 without authorization if it will help solve a problem for a customer; line-level employees can spend up to $2,000.)

10. To use guest incident action forms to record and communicate every incident of guest dissatisfaction. Every employee is empowered to resolve the problem and to prevent a repeat occurrence.

11. To be responsible for uncompromising levels of cleanliness.

12. To smile, always be on stage, and maintain positive eye contact. Ritz recommends vocabulary, including words and phrases such as "Good morning," "Certainly," "I'll be happy to," and "My pleasure."

13. To be the hotel's ambassador and always talk positively about it.

14. To escort guests rather than pointing out directions.

15. To know general information about the hotel in order to be able to answer guest inquiries directly.

16. To answer the phone within three rings, to do it with a smile, to ask the caller's permission before putting him or her on hold, to not screen calls, and to resolve the call without transferring the party if at all possible.

17. To have an immaculate uniform and grooming.

18. To know his or her role in emergency situations.

19. To notify the supervisor immediately of hazards, injuries, or needed equipment or assistance; to conserve energy and to keep property and equipment in good condition.

20. To protect the hotel's assets.

Ritz-Carlton points out that fully 96% of its employees identified "excellence in guest services" as a top priority, even though 3,000 employees have been with Ritz-Carlton for less than three years.

INTERVIEW WITH RITZ-CARLTON

Q First, let me say that I received all your information, and it was very helpful. Most of it was familiar to me because we use it in our seminars. My first question is this: Tell me about Ritz Carlton's philosophy regarding customer service.

A Basically, our philosophy is that we are ladies and gentlemen serving ladies and gentlemen.

Q You do whatever it takes to make the customer satisfied?

A Yes, we are willing to move heaven and earth to make our customers satisfied. Our employees are allowed and indeed are required to break away from their routine and to apply some sort of immediate positive action if the customer's requirements are not being met.

Q Ritz has the most important aspect that I have ever noticed in all the mottos and mission statements that I've reviewed. I'm talking about number 8 of your 20 basics, specifically, that any employee who receives a guest complaint owns the complaint.

A Yes. That provides for immediate and complete resolution of any and every problem. Basically, when things go wrong, and they will, the individual employee is responsible to apply some sort of immediate positive action. The employee is expected to break away from routine duties, to apply some sort of immediate positive reaction, and then snap back to the routine duties. Our employees are managing customer complaints. All employees are managers.

Q I understand. I have noticed that a great many companies talk about empowerment, but Ritz is one of the very few companies that actually enable and expect their people to act in an empowered way.

A We try. Anything that can happen in life can happen in a hotel. We are open 24 hours a day, and employees can

223

find themselves in situations that involve a great deal of ambiguity. We give our people the confidence and the freedom and authority to satisfy the customer. To some degree, hotels are nothing more than great big job shops. Every customer presents something new and different, and so we give our employees the flexibility to deal with that.

Q Tell me a little more about your training programs. How often do you train? What do you do that's different?

A People are trained in a triple role concept at the Ritz. First, our people are trained on how to be a lady or a gentleman, and that's done by an upper manager of the hotel. This training starts during the first hour of employment and it lasts for about two days. That's the hospitality and ambassador part of the training. After new employees complete that successfully, they start to master the procedures of their jobs. Once they complete that, they are introduced to managing for quality: how to plan for quality and how to improve quality. So those three areas of training deal with the three roles that Ritz employees learn to play. The ladies-and-gentlemen training starts in the very first hour and continues through the first two days of employment. All new recruits get that. Then, for 60 days, they go through what we call training certification. Afterwards, and this is ongoing, Ritz has management for quality. A unique part of our training is that every day we devote five minutes at the beginning of each shift to a lineup where we do two things: We reinforce our values, and we introduce some new elements or aspects of the training. So, we do a lot of training every day.

Q Obviously, it is ongoing.

A It is not necessarily done in a classroom.

Q It could happen on the job?

A Absolutely. Training takes place in the work area or else standing in an environment where individuals are very comfortable.

Q I have noticed something different, at least at the Cleveland Ritz-Carlton. I have never seen it in other organizations. On Friday, the people in senior management actually hand out the paychecks so that they can put faces with names. Do you consider that important?

A Yes. It is very important to know who your employees are and to know something about them. I can't say that this procedure is standard at every Ritz, but it does follow the values of the company.

Q I don't know about turnover in your industry or at Ritz-Carlton. Is your turnover lower than the industry average?

A Substantially. Industry turnover can be 60 to 100% and we have it down to under 30%.

Q Wow! By way of introduction to my next question, let me say that all corporations have an advertising budget, but when asked about their training budget, they may tell you they have one, but it is not specific. I am trying to find out if the best corporations all have a budget for training.

A I can just tell you that on the average we spend about 120 hours per employee providing some sort of transfer of information. Again, that is not classroom training. We have those first three days and the training certification and those five minutes every day of lineup. It adds up to about 120 hours.

Q Do you have a number written down somewhere that tells you what you are going to spend next year on training?

A Right.

Q You guys know what you are going to spend in the coming year on training. Great. That's as much as I want to know. What do you do to motivate your employees? Is there anything special that you do?

A Yes. We realize that when things go wrong, it is because they were planned that way, maybe inadvertently. So we don't blame the workers for not doing their best.

Q It's like always looking for the things that are right. That's what author Ken Blanchard says.

A Right. So the point we are making is that you really have to manage for quality with your upper managers and plan for things to go right. It's very much like the old days, when there was the craft concept. Even though the craft concept related more to products, the fact remains that the people were involved in the planning of the product. They made the product they were going to use. They were their own customer. They were involved in all the activities. In other words, if step number 11 was creating a problem for step 24, they detected it and corrected it before it reached the customer. They eliminated problems before they occurred. So, by involving the workers in planning for quality and by having more variety in their work, what results is that workers are more involved. That is one of the main ingredients in workers being motivated. Like managers, workers are involved in the planning. We don't use the conventional approach, which is to give everybody a goal and urge them to meet it. We feel that is futile when the problem is in the planning. I think the major motivation is provided when we involve workers in planning the work, not just in carrying out the action.

Q What makes you the best in your business, and what do you think will keep you there?

A Well, I think there are a couple of things. First of all, as anyone can understand, especially in the luxury hotel business, we realize that the customer's expectations extend beyond the functional. What we are talking about is really a psychological thing. We have to really understand who our customers are and what they want, need, or expect.

And then we have to deliver those psychological expectations along with the functional expectations. Great service businesses do these things well. Ritz has beautiful surroundings. I think we do that as well as anyone. We have warm, caring employees. I think we do that as well as anyone. We have timely delivery. I think we do that as well if not a little better than anyone, and that includes consistency from hotel to hotel. I think the thing we do the best is that our people recognize our regular guests. The Ritz really remembers.

Q Therefore, using your database and everything related to it, the information is right there when the employee needs it.

A Yes. The main things are the psychological aspect and the fact that we have a good memory. There are other aspects, of course. We are good contractually. But I think that when it comes down to it, the psychological aspect is what makes the Ritz-Carlton excel.

Q What are the one or two most important qualities that you look for in potential employees?

A We look for people who genuinely care about people.

Q In a word, you are talking about attitude.

A Yes. Spontaneous behavior. We look for employees who would naturally share our values.

Q Would you summarize the most important thing about your policies regarding customer service. Is it basically, like you said, just do whatever it takes to make the customer happy, to exceed their expectations?

A Well, I could recite the credo, but I would summarize it for you in these words: beautiful surroundings, recognition of regular guests, warm and caring employees, consistency, and on-time delivery.

Q There's just one point I would like you to clarify. I know that most hotels, such as Holiday Inns, are either franchises or are run by management companies, so that different management companies run different Holiday Inns. Does your group out of Atlanta run and manage all the Ritz-Carltons?

A There are one or two exceptions, where we inherited a hotel run by others, but almost all of our 35 Ritz-Carltons are managed by our group.

Q So, you are one single management company running the Ritz-Carlton rather than 8 or 10 different ones.

A We are a hotel management company who runs only one high-grade brand. We specialize.

SOUTHWEST AIRLINES

f I had to pick my absolute most favorite company of all, Southwest Airlines would be it. Not only does Southwest do a terrific job, but everyone at the company has a lot of fun doing it!

As I write this book, Southwest is the only U.S. airline in the history of aviation to have been profitable 23 years in a row. It is the only airline that made money every one of the past five years. Southwest has several times won the Triple Crown, the airline industry's highest rating in customer satisfaction.

Here is the amazing part. Southwest has done this despite the fact that it has no first-class section. It has no assigned seating. It loads people like cattle. It has no serious food service. It has no extended baggage handling. It has no amenities for the customer whatsoever. In spite of all these disadvantages, Southwest is still number one. Why? Southwest Airlines exceeds customer expectations.

First of all, Southwest has one of the best on-time records in the industry. Second, as of this writing, it has never had a crash (on second thought, make that fact number one).

But there's much more! What also makes Southwest Airlines great is their attitude. When Herb Kelleher hires employees, he looks for three things that he considers a must: (1) enthusiasm; (2) a sense of humor; and (3) a great attitude. Frequent flyers are asked to help hire other employees, on the grounds that customers know what they want and don't want.

Southwest encourages people to ask for forgiveness rather than for permission. The employee handbook has been shortened from 500 pages to 60 pages. Managers are encouraged to think on their feet.

Southwest encourages laughter and humor, and it hires only individuals who are able to laugh at themselves. Its people are expected to be enthusiastic and sincere and to use common sense. Employees are allowed to break the rules in the interest of customer service. Employees are expected to go above and beyond for customers.

The CEO, Herb Kelleher, has done some amazing things. His people just adore him. He is said to know almost all 14,000 people by first name. He never says "I" but instead gives credit to everybody else. He recognizes employees for helping other employees. Employee turnover is 6%, one of the lowest in the industry.

People are cross trained, and it's not unusual to see a vice president working at the gate. Pilots hire other pilots, which makes the original pilots accountable. All this is part of the culture. Southwest calls it "crazy like a fox."

Another outstanding feature is that Southwest people overwhelm their customers with incredible humor. Here are some of the things people at Southwest do.

At the ticket counter, your might be asked to take off your shoes to see how many holes you have in your socks. The person with the most holes gets a drink coupon for the flight. Or you might be asked you to take out your wallet and count your credit cards. The person with the most credit cards gets a coupon for a drink.

When you are on the plane, you might hear the pilot say on the PA system, "Hello, this is the pilot of Flight such-and-such. We have a little problem. It's nothing to get worried about, but our plane will be delayed due to a small baggage problem. Our automatic bag smasher is broken. So we are personally smashing all your bags by hand on the tarmac. Please be patient." Of course, people laugh.

Then a pilot might come on the PA in a tiny, high-pitched voice, saying, "Hi, my name is Bobbie, and I'll be your pilot today. We're going to go *real* high, and real, real fast, too." People start to laugh. They can't believe they are having this much fun on a plane.

My favorite story is about a guy running to the gate, all disheveled and sweating. He's angry. He is very late for his plane. There is one seat left on the plane. Inside the plane, with the help of a couple of passengers, the flight attendants have put the smallest flight attendant into the overhead compartment.

The passenger comes down the aisle, huffing and puffing. All the other passengers can hardly wait for what's going to happen. When the guy opens the overhead compartment to put his briefcase in it, the flight attendant hops out and says, "May I take this for you, sir?" Can you imagine the look on his face?

What is happening here? The employees are having fun. The passengers are having fun. The employees meet their deadlines, they meet their goals, and they add a little fun to it. Everybody wins, and everybody has fun. Now that's the way to run a business. Let the people enjoy what they do every day.

What is the result of all this? Southwest has built incredible employee loyalty. Its people want to please not only the customer but also senior management. This loyalty exists because people have been given latitude. They are not afraid of losing their jobs or of making the wrong decision. There is a spirit of total teamwork.

Does this take time? Absolutely. Will it happen overnight? Never.

The mission of Southwest Airlines is dedication to the highest quality of customer service delivered with a sense of warmth, friendliness, individual pride, and company spirit.

Southwest's mission statement says, "We are committed to provide our employees a stable work environment with equal opportunity for learning and personal growth. Creativity and innovation are encouraged for improving the effectiveness of Southwest Airlines. Above all, employees will be provided the same concern, respect, and caring attitude within the organization that they are expected to share externally with every Southwest customer."

INTERVIEW WITH SOUTHWEST AIRLINES

Q What is Southwest's philosophy regarding customer service?

A Well, for what is most important, we can go to our mission statement, which says that we are dedicated to the highest quality of customer service, delivered with a sense of warmth, friendliness, individual pride, and company spirit.

Q I see you are prepared. It is right in front of you.

A That's right.

Q Tell me a little about your training programs. What do you do? How often? Is it ongoing?

A We have continual training in customer service. The cus-tomer is so important at Southwest Airlines that we capital-ize it. We are always reinforcing customer service. We are always modeling great examples of customer service, which we do through our awards program.

Q Tell me a bit more about modeling.

A We show examples of outstanding customer service through our awards program and through our internal publications. We are always doing that.

Q So you use examples of problems that happened and how your people took care of them.

A We are always holding up our employees and applauding them for their great customer service. So, that is one of the ways we continually reinforce the importance of customer service.

Q What I notice when I fly is that Southwest really lets its people do whatever they want to do.

A Exactly. We recognize that the needs of our customers are all very different. People are traveling for quite a variety of reasons, and so people have very different needs. Some people are concentrating on on-time performance because they are traveling to a business meeting. A traveler might be going to a funeral. Somebody else might be going to a wedding. People travel for all sorts of different reasons, and we try to accommodate those individual needs.

Q Every company has an advertising budget. I'm not asking for an exact number, but do you have a budget for train-ing?

A Sure. We have a whole department, several departments.

Q What do you do to motivate your employees, to keep morale high, in addition to the things you mentioned?

A Let me give you an example. Every time a customer writes a congratulatory letter about an employee, Herb will write to that employee and say, "Here's a copy of the customer letter we received about you. Way to go! Hat's off! Keep up the great work." It has been that type of reinforcement that keeps employees motivated.

Q Based on the industry numbers, you are the only airline to be profitable 23 years in a row. You have won the airline industry's Triple Crown a number of times. You don't do what some airlines do, advertising that you are the best airline for the first five miles. What makes you the best in the business, and what do you think will keep you there?

A We do not look at ourselves as an airline with great customer service. We are a great customer service organization that just happens to be in the airline business.

Q I like that. I really like that a lot. What are the qualities that you look for in a potential employee? I know what Herb said in some of the meetings, but I'm curious about what is thought corporatewide.

A We certainly look for the type of employee who wants to serve the customer, for someone who puts the customer's needs first.

Q What do you look for in the employee? Do you look for certain attributes in that person who sits in front of you or in front of the desk?

A Right. When we hire, we are looking for people who view their personal interests as not being the most important thing. Instead, we want people who see how important the needs of the customers are. One of the things we look for is an employee with a sense of humor. We want people who don't take themselves too seriously. Let me clarify that. We are looking for employees who—besides not taking themselves too seriously—take their job seriously.

Q So, in other words, you want them to have fun and have the right attitude?

A We want them to have fun enjoying their work.

Q And you encourage fun. I see it all the time.

A   Absolutely. It is the best part of our culture, too.

Q   Can you tell me a little about your policies regarding customer service? Do you have any policies in place besides "just do it" and things like that?

A   That's right. We definitely train our employees. There are definite policies, but an employee will never get in trouble for erring on the side of the customer.

Q   Wow! That's pretty cool. You almost never hear that.

A   We are looking out for the best interests of our customers.

15

The Future of Customer Service

As I see it, the customer service industry will be dominated by smart people in smart companies doing the right things. The companies that refuse to do the right things will simply not survive.

For an example, look at Kmart or Sears. Many moons ago, Sears was the number one retailer in the world. But they lost their focus. They started investing in a lot of other different businesses, including insurance, and they lost sight of the fact that they were a retailer and in the business of customer service. Sears subsequently sold almost all its various businesses and returned to focusing on what it does best. As a result, Sears stock has improved, the customer base has stopped eroding, and the company has returned to a respectable level.

Kmart faces the same situation. Kmart has gone off in many different directions and has stopped focusing on what it does best: discount retailing. Then Wal-Mart came in. Typically, if you go into any discount department store and ask where the automotive section is, someone will point you in the general direction. If you go to Wal-Mart and ask the same question, an employee will escort you there.

The future belongs to service companies that organize their systems and train their people to give truly outstanding service. Let me give you an example that blew me away.

This happened at Target, a discount department store. I was in the shampoo section, looking for a certain brand. An employee was stocking one of the shelves, and I asked her if Target had that brand. She looked around for about two minutes, and she couldn't find it.

I said, "That's okay. Thanks, anyway." She was very nice. About 10 minutes later, when I was in a totally different department of the store, I felt a tap on my shoulder. I turned around, and there was the employee from the shampoo section.

She said, "Sir, I found the shampoo for you." Now, is this great training? Absolutely.

The strength of an individual store depends on its general manager, who has the authority to run the store as he or she sees fit. If the manager is weak, service will be poor. When you find a strong store with excellent service, you know the manager is doing everything necessary to see that employees are trained and that they do what it takes to satisfy customers.

I think that automobile dealerships are going to have a rude awakening very soon. Lexus is giving its customers whatever they want to make them happy. Saturn has a very similar policy. No hassle.

Now H. Wayne Huizenga, who heads Republic Industries, is coming in and revolutionizing the automobile dealership industry overnight. Look at what he has done just since November 1996.

He bought two car-rental companies: Alamo, which services weekend and leisure customers, and National, which focuses on business and corporate rental. Then Huizenga bought more than 275 new-car dealers. In less than a year, he went from owning zero dealerships to having the largest group of new-car dealerships in the United States. When one of his rental cars hits about 10,000 miles or so, the car is transferred to AutoNation USA, which is a superstore of used cars. Huizenga will take you from your first car to your last, and he will have you as a customer for personal and business cars, whether they are new, used, or rented. This guy is going to corner the market.

This scenario will happen in every industry. You will see one person change the market and force competitors to do a better job.

The key factor is strong competition. Go to Orlando, Florida, and try to find a bad hotel on Disney property. You won't be able to do it because the competition is so fierce that it raises the bar to new levels.

So, in my opinion, the issue really comes down to service. Read Bill Gates' book, *The Road Ahead,* especially the paperback version. It tells how the Internet is going to change the world, and how the PC revolution is nothing compared to the Internet revolution. I agree.

When *At Your Service* first comes out, this view might be fresh and new. But down the road, I think you are going to see everybody sharing this idea. All companies will be going in the direction of unbelievable service because of the impact of the Internet.

The customer will go to the Internet's Web pages and find all the information necessary to make a smart purchase, including the cost and the suggested retail price of products. Then the customer will be able to say to the retailer or the business, "This is what I want to do."

This capability means the customer is going to win—and the smart businesses will win, too!

Wal-Mart changed everything when it stopped using brokers and went direct to manufacturers. Wal-Mart can track its inventory via satellite and can ship inventory directly to whatever location it's needed, all without distributors and brokers. As a result, customer prices are lower. Some of the vendors obviously took a beating in their gross margins. They sold their products for less and made less profit. But they made it up in volume.

Small businesses are becoming big businesses. For example, OfficeMax started with one idea and one location, in Mayfield Heights, Ohio, and today it has become one of the largest discount office-supply stores. Home Depot and a number of other companies have done much the same thing.

The megastores, megadealers, mega-anythings are the ones that are going to change the face of business. And the Internet will help create the new business environment.

We have no idea where the future will take us. When I talk about the future, I'm talking about a very short period of time—10 years. The Internet is going to totally change the way we do business and the way we communicate with each other.

When the first PC came out in 1981, who would have thought that in just 17 years almost every workstation and every home would have one? Well, the Internet revolution will make the PC revolution look like kindergarten.

With all that technology, we will still need to have great customer service.

I think that, in the midst of this incredible technological change, we need to introduce a concept that goes back half a century, to the 1940s. I'm talking about the concept of the general store, which I discussed in my introduction.

Of course, there are unreasonable customers. In fact, most businesses find that about one percent of their customers are unreasonable or simply a pain in the neck.

But most customer concerns are legitimate.

I think companies are using technology in a way that hurts them and alienates their customers. A perfect example is voice mail. For example, if you try to call any computer manufacturer or support vendor, you have to go through voice mail, 1,900 different buttons, and sometimes you can't even get out.

This approach is wrong. We will have to go back to using people and using the technology to enable those people to do a better job of serving customers, with innovations such as CD-ROMs and interactive software.

General Electric is a great example of a company that is using technology to help its customer support people help the customer, and to make the customer want to stay a GE customer. If I buy a GE appliance and get unbelievably good service, then when I need another new appliance I will always think first of GE.

If you are really happy with a vendor or a company, if that company really goes out of its way to show you that it cares, if that company proves that it puts you the customer first, and if that company makes you feel that you were taken care of in the right way—then you the consumer will stay with that company and continue to buy its products.

That is the future. Good systems, well-trained people, and policies and procedures that benefit the customer.

To Sum It All Up

I go back to the golden rule: treat people the way *you* want to be treated. Or you could subscribe to the platinum rule, set down in a recent book by Tony Alessandra: Treat people the way *they* want to be treated.

So if we put together the right company policies, the right people, and the right attitude—wow! Together we can create incredible customer service.

As you read this book, whether you are an owner, manager, employee, or just a frustrated consumer, I hope it's clear that the answers are not complicated. The best companies have made customer service simple and have kept it simple. Good customer service doesn't have to be complicated or difficult to achieve. It's merely a never-ending struggle to improve and to stay focused on the two most important areas: *your people and your customers!* Highlight the important points in this book, read it again, and learn—not from me, but from the companies that have done it right! We can all be the best when *we decide that we really, really want to.*

I hope you enjoyed my walk through many companies. Again, I didn't write *At Your Service* to be mean or spiteful. We all have incredible stories about bad customer service. I thought it would be fun to put them in a book so that we could laugh at ourselves and laugh at the companies. And then we can try to make a world with better customer service—and have fun doing it!

Thank you.

Customer Behavior Test

Thank you for taking the time to read this book. *For those of you who are standing in a bookstore and opening to this page first:* WHAT DO YOU THINK THIS IS—A LIBRARY?

The official *At Your Service* customer behavior test
See if you act properly in your quest for goods and services.

1. It's midnight and you are checking into a hotel:
   ___ a. You stand quietly in line while the night clerk stays on the line with 1-900-spankme.
   ___ b. You demand the presidential suite, even if the commander in chief is in town.
   ___ c. You accept the broom closet, grateful that nobody has been nasty to you.
   ___ d. You have no reservation, but in a confident tone you say, "Reservation for Smith," and you scowl until they find you a room.

Correct answer: d. There must be 3 million Smiths in the United States, so the chances are you beat one of them to this hotel.

2. You go to a superstore to buy a television for your mobile home:
   ___ a. You go in to buy a 12-inch portable and you come out with the 60-inch radiation special.
   ___ b. You opt for no payments until 1999.
   ___ c. The salesperson is so good that you buy the 12-piece set of living-room furniture (and you live in a mobile home).

Correct answer: b. With any luck, by 1999 you will die or move to Tahiti, and your television time will be free.

3. When you rent a car on vacation:

___ a. You buy all the extra insurance, and when you feel the clerk is ready to celebrate being employee of the week, you say, "Never mind. I don't want it."

___ b. When the clerk asks you where you are lodging, you say, "I'm not going anywhere. I'm staying in the car. Why do you think I rented it?"

___ c. You rent a Chevy and ask the clerk for directions to the Chevy stock-car race.

Correct answer: b. Because you're living in the car, you can bring it back with really low mileage.

4. At the post office:

___ a. You wait patiently behind a customer who wants to see every "Love" stamp ever issued, and you see the postal clerk reach for an Uzi under the counter.

___ b. You anticipate that whatever special mailing request you have, the answer will be, "Not at this branch."

___ c. You marvel that the workforce can move so slowly that they cannot be seen by conventional motion detectors.

Correct answer: a. When some of the customers have been mowed down, the line will be shorter.

5. When you go to the airport:

___ a. You arrive early because you expect to be stuck at the security gate behind a World War II hero with so much shrapnel in his body that he sets off all the metal detectors.

___ b. The baggage handler says, "Portland, Oregon, or Portland, Maine—what's the difference?" and you think twice about checking your bags.

c. You pick up your grandmother at the baggage claim exit, and she has to jump into your car as you slow down to 20 miles an hour so that you can keep the traffic patrol people happy.

Correct answer: b. If you check you bags, you have a 50% chance they will reach the right city, which is pretty good odds for an airline.

6. At the bank:

    a. When you ask how late the bank will be open, the teller requires three forms of identification before answering your question.

    b. While you wait for the one working teller, you admire the lobby, newly remodeled to the tune of $2.5 million.

    c. You apply for the 3.9% introductory offer credit card, which in two months will revert back to a competitive 27.9% interest.

Correct answer: c: Get the card because the easiest way to pay off a MasterCard is to put it on your Visa.

7. At the car dealer:

    a. After you have shopped the competition and signed the best deal you can make, you hear your salesman calling his wife and telling her, "Book the trip to Hawaii!"

    b. When you take your car in for service that is covered by warranty, they charge you $300 for your cup of coffee.

    c. You find out the name of the general manager at another dealership, let it slip that he's your cousin, and then watch the price come down.

Correct answer: a. So what if you pay $35,000 for a Yugo? For another $5,000, they will throw in a tow truck.

Customer Behavior Test

Scoring

Each correct answer is worth 5 points.

If you scored 30–35 points, you probably do well on the TV show *Jeopardy,* meaning you have way too much time on your hands.

If you scored 20–25 points, you are probably disputing our correct answers versus your correct answers, meaning you have way too much time on your hands.

If you scored 10–15 points, you did as well as the college athlete who answers "d" for every question on his entrance exam but passes because he correctly lists his height at 7′2″.

If you scored 0–5 points, you are the customer that every retail shark is looking for. Do not leave your house.

This test was composed by Jon Lief, one of the funniest people in his zip code.

About the Author

Hal Becker is an internationally known expert on sales and customer service. He makes more than 170 presentations a year to hundreds of companies and organizations, including IBM, B.F. Goodrich, Ford, ADT, Bank One, KeyCorp, Blue Cross, AT&T, New York Life, Hormel Foods and American Greetings.

At the age of 22, Hal became the number one salesperson in a national sales force of 11,000 for Xerox Corporation. Six years later, in 1983, the same passion and energy helped him survive terminal cancer just months after he launched his company, Direct Opinions. Direct Opinions was one of the first customer-service telemarketing firms. It now conducts more than 2 million calls per year nationwide.

In 1990 Hal sold Direct Opinions in order to devote time to presenting lectures and seminars around the world and to promoting his national bestseller, *Can I Have Five Minutes of Your Time?* This book, now in its tenth printing, is used by many corporations as their sales bible.

Hal has been featured in many publications, including *The Wall Street Journal, Nation's Business,* and hundreds of newspapers and radio and television stations worldwide.

He founded The Cancer Hotline of Cleveland, a nonprofit telephone service that provides support and information for cancer patients and their families. The Cancer Hotline is supported from the proceeds of his books. Hal can be reached at 1-800-253-0466 or www.Halbecker.Com.

Index